How to
Write Great
Screenplays

Other titles for creative writers from How To Books

LIKELY STORIES
*Fabulous, inspirational, chuckleworthy and deeply instructive tales about
creative writing as told to the author by his ubiquitous Guru*
Hugh Scott
Whitbread winning author

**HOW TO WRITE A CHILDREN'S PICTURE BOOK
– AND GET IT PUBLISHED**
Andrea Shavick

HOW TO WRITE FOR TELEVISION
A guide to writing and selling successful TV scripts
William Smethurst

365 WAYS TO GET YOU WRITING
Inspiration and advice for creative writers on a daily basis
Jane Cooper

HOW TO WRITE YOUR FIRST NOVEL
Sophie King

THE FIVE-MINUTE WRITER
Exercise and inspiration in creative writing in five minutes a day
Maureen Geraghty

Write or phone for a catalogue to:

How To Books
Spring Hill House
Spring Hill Road
Begbroke
Oxford OX5 1RX
Tel. 01865 375794

Or email: info@howtobooks.co.uk

Visit our website www.howtobooks.co.uk
to find out more about us and our books

Like our Facebook page How To Books & Spring Hill

Read our books online www.howto.co.uk

How to
Write Great
Screenplays
and get them
into production

LINDA M JAMES

howtobooks

Published by How To Books Ltd,
Spring Hill House, Spring Hill Road,
Begbroke, Oxford OX5 1RX, United Kingdom.
Tel: (01865) 375794. Fax: (01865) 379162.
info@howtobooks.co.uk
www.howtobooks.co.uk

How To Books greatly reduce the carbon footprint of their books by sourcing their
typesetting and printing in the UK.

First edition 2009
Reprinted 2010
Reprinted 2012

British Library Cataloguing in Publication Data
A catalogue record for this book is available from the British Library

ISBN 978 1 84528 307 0

Produced for How To Books by Deer Park Productions, Tavistock, Devon
Typeset by PDQ Typesetting, Newcastle-under-Lyme, Staffs.
Printed and bound by Bell & Bain Ltd, Glasgow

Contents

Acknowledgements

We would like to thank solicitor Stephen Aucutt for his help with clarifying problems over copyright and registration.

We would also like to thank the legal company Reed Smith Richards Butler for permission to reproduce their information on options and assignments, Crossleys Solicitors for permission to reproduce the sample option agreement and the attorneys Lichter, Grossman, Nichols & Adler, Inc. for permission to reproduce the opening scene from *The Matrix*.

For screenwriters everywhere

Pictures tell the story

Prologue

Screenwriting is a fascinating process, but it requires talent, technical skill and tenacity. You must have all three to succeed in such a competitive industry. I can't give you talent, but I can give you the technical skills you'll need to produce a great script, and through its creation the confidence to market your work until you achieve success.

Remember that film is a visual medium, so when you write a screenplay think in pictures; pictures that tell a story through images that linger in the mind, through dialogue that's believable and concise, and through creative description.

Many people start writing their screenplay from an initial (often great) idea, then flounder half way through. This reminds me of the story of the man who gets on a bus and when the conductor asks him where he's going, he says, 'I don't know.' The bus conductor answers: 'Then you'll never get there, mate.' You need to know your destination.

As a writer and writing tutor, I realise how daunting writing a first (or even a fifth) script can be. This book will simplify the writing process by giving you clear, thought-provoking explanations, examples of good writing and exercises to help you consolidate everything you've learned. It will also tell you of websites where you can download hundreds of screenplays to accelerate that learning.

This book has been written to help you stand out from the crowd.

Alfred Hitchcock

'What is drama, after all, but life with the dull bits cut out.'

The Importance of Preparation

TEN POWERFUL QUESTIONS

Before you start writing your screenplay save yourself months – or even years – of frustration by answering these questions:

1. What is your story about? (In a couple of sentences – see the discussion of loglines in Chapter 9.)

2. What genre is it? (Comedy? Horror? Thriller? Drama? See the discussion of 'Genre' in Chapter 10.)

3. What's the mood of the film? For example, edgy/comic/mysterious/poignant/frightening, etc.

4. What time period does the film cover? (A day, a month, a year, many years or centuries? Would it matter if you changed the time period?)

5. Who is the main character? (The protagonist.) Who is opposing him or her? (The antagonist.)

6. In what order are you going to tell your story? Sequentially, with one event linked to another in a sequence of time? Or are you going to jump back and forth in time through flashbacks? (Obviously, more complicated.)

7. How many locations do you need to illustrate these time periods? Do you need them all? Why?

8. What conflicts are there in your story? (What do your characters want? What obstacles are you going to give them?)

9. How are your major characters going to overcome these obstacles to reach their goal?

10. Do you have a subplot? (A minor plot which relates in some way to the main plot. Some scripts have more than one, but don't make life too hard for yourself.)

To show you how effective these questions can be in writing an exciting, tight screenplay, I'm going to use this list to explore how I wrote my psychological thriller called *White Witch*.

1. Richard, an attractive ex-painter, travels to a Jamaican sugar plantation in 1830 to escape his past, but finds life even more disturbing as the plantation is run by a beautiful obeah woman (white witch) who's looking for a new lover. Richard is seduced by her, but eventually, he manages to find the courage to help the slaves and escape.

2. This is a historical, psychological thriller.

3. The mood is dark. (It could hardly be anything else with such a story.)

4. The script covers a period of 20 years.

5. The protagonist is Richard; the antagonist is the white witch and her obeahism.

6. The story is not told sequentially. The script starts in 1856 when Richard is middle-aged and moves back to his life on the sugar plantation in the 1830s, then moves forward again.

7. I used one location in the present (a lecture hall); one location in the past (Richard's brother's bedroom, where he's burning); all the other scenes take place in Jamaica.

8. There are numerous conflicts and twists in the story; Richard is desperately trying to escape the guilt he feels about his young brother's death (first obstacle), but going to Jamaica makes his life far more complicated and dangerous (second obstacle). Two women fall in love/lust with him (many more obstacles). Richard is desperate to leave the plantation once he discovers the appalling things that happen there but, of course, the white witch stops him in numerous ways.

9. Richard has to learn that he must change himself before he can help the slaves on the plantation. This will be the only way he will achieve any peace in his life and find a means to escape.

10. I have a number of subplots which reflect back to the main plot through the themes of guilt, witchcraft and oppression of people.

As you will see from point number 8, Richard has a strong goal and a strong adversity in the white witch. It is vitally important for screenwriters to create a strong goal for their protagonist and to have one or more people (antagonists) who try to stop him from achieving that goal. It is also important that the audience identify with the hero for then they bond with him and engage with his struggle.

IDENTIFYING WITH THE HERO

One way to make an audience identify with the hero is to show a trauma in their past. My protagonist, an artist called Richard, feels incredible guilt because his young brother burned to death while he was painting and listening to music. He travels to Jamaica in an effort to forget the past but, of course, it travels with him. Once we know about Richard's guilt, we become interested in him and concerned about his future.

Here's another example of how the past can affect the present life of a character.

Also not an adventurous person but buttoned-up.

James is an overly cautious man, afraid to enjoy life. To stop the audience finding him irritating, we must show early in the script why he's become so cautious. Here's a way to do it: when James was 13 his father lost all the family money by gambling. His mother died and he and his alcoholic father lived in poverty until James left home. Consequently, we understand why he is frightened to take risks – they could lead to a similar disaster. This backstory makes us empathize with James so we want him to overcome his fears. Of course, we now escalate James' problems by introducing a character (the antagonist) who challenges him so much that he is forced out of his caution to achieve something he never thought possible.

We also identify with people who are being unjustly treated. The theme of injustice has a universal appeal in all cultures (and has spawned many Hollywood films). Once we identify with people's problems we are hooked; we worry about them and so must continue watching to see what happens to them. This worry creates tension, especially when we know that a character's actions are likely to make life even more difficult for him.

Of course, as a writer, you *must* escalate the problems your protagonist faces so the audience can't imagine how he can possibly get himself out of the terrible situation he finds himself in.

CREATING INTERESTING CHARACTERS

When you're creating characters, think in contrasts: in age, gender, attitude and social status. This will help you create interesting people.

Answer these questions:

1. Where were your characters born and when?

2. Do they like the way they look?

3. What are their parents like? If they are still alive, do they relate to them or not? If they don't, why not?

4. Were they well educated or not? Were they happy and popular in school or not? Why?

5. What work do they do? Do they enjoy it or not?

6. Do they have siblings? Do they get on with them? If not, why not?

7. How do they dress? (Classic/casual/elegant/hippie, etc.)

8. How do they speak? Have they got an unusual speech pattern? Do they interrupt people/listen carefully/only listen

occasionally/speak spontaneously or after some thought? If none of these, how?

9. How do they move? Are they awkward/confident/hesitant/ graceful or none of these?

10. What do they like about themselves? What do they dislike?

11. What is their major character flaw? How are you going to use it in your plotting?

12. Have they ever suffered a trauma in the past? How does this affect them now?

13. Have they got a favourite place? (This could be a den in their house or a country.)

14. What do they hate/love doing in their leisure time?

15. How would you describe their personality?

16. What do they really want? What are they prepared to do to get it?

17. Are they active, i.e. do they have the energy to achieve their goal? (This doesn't need to be physical energy – elderly characters may have a burning mental power that controls the people around them.)

To make us care about your characters, you must make them believable. There must be a consistency of action, dialogue and reaction with which we identify.

Audiences always want to know why someone behaves or acts or speaks in a certain way. As long as the writer shows the audience credible reasons, we will accept even villainous characters like Hannibal Lector. (Did you know that Hannibal's sister was eaten by soldiers when he was a young boy?)

> **N.B.** The bottom line for writing any character is credibility. It's vital to know what motivates each character to create fascinating, flawed people.

EXERCISE

Write out character biographies of all your major characters. By writing biographies you will discover exactly how each character thinks, moves and acts, i.e. they will become three-dimensional.

Robbie the rest of England is a foreign country to him

Outlines, Synopses and Treatments

A great deal of confusion exists about the meaning of these three terms, so I will explain them clearly and simply.

OUTLINES

An outline is like a very short story. You write it to crystallize what your story is about. It's your map. It helps you clearly summarize your story. You write an outline so you can find the head and the heart of your story.

Often people start with a theme that suggests a universal truth such as: 'power corrupts'; 'love hurts'; 'betrayal destroys'; 'injustice should be fought', etc.

The theme is what the film is 'about'. If you can find a theme that is both interesting and universal, you are on the road to creating a great screenplay. Once you have your theme, start writing your outline, but remember this outline is personal; you don't need to send it out to people (unlike the synopsis and treatment). People often use the word 'outline' when they really mean synopsis.

> **N.B**. *If you can't write the outline, then you don't know what your story is about. If this is the case, work on another idea.*

STEP OUTLINES

The way to ensure that your idea has enough 'legs', i.e. enough dramatic tension, suspense and an interesting plot, is to write a step outline of that idea. A step outline is basically a scene-by-scene breakdown of your story. You don't usually send a step outline out – it's a tool to help you structure your script.

Of course, many people don't want to do this because this is where most of the work is done – it's much more exciting to start writing the script immediately. The problem with such spontaneity is that your idea is likely to disappear as you slump into confused despondency. As I mentioned in Chapter 1, all the preparation you do before you write will stop you from burning out halfway through your script because you have no idea where it's going.

WRITING A STEP OUTLINE

The golden rule when writing step outlines: if a scene doesn't inform us about the characters or drive the story along in some way then it shouldn't be there.

When writing a step outline list each scene in your future screenplay, describing what takes place in it. This allows you to see how the structure of the film is working. It also gives you an opportunity to start cutting unnecessary details before you begin. A good step outline is like the skeleton of your script; if it's strong, it will support 110 pages of writing.

For example, say you're going to write about a jazz singer who discovers her boyfriend is having an affair with a dancer (the theme of 'love hurts'). You want to hook the audience immediately so you write as follows:

1. Carl's bedroom. Bella shimmies into the room to find her rival Sonia in bed with her man. She yanks Sonia out of the bed and hits her across the face. Carl is livid.

2. Nightclub. Bella sings to an appreciative audience. From the back of the room Carl watches her. He blows her a kiss.

3. Street. Carl leaves the club. Alone.

4. Nightclub. On stage Bella looks panic-stricken by Carl's sudden disappearance. She stops halfway through a number and marches off the stage. The audience is stunned.

You continue writing like this until you have mapped out every scene.

Making changes

However, remember that this step outline isn't final. As you write the script, your scenes will change. Then why bother writing one, I hear you cry? Because a step outline will show you clearly where the flaws in your characterization and plotting occur. You can move scenes around to see how different your script could become.

Let's do that with the above 'steps'. How would our reaction to Bella change if I opened the script with the second scene? For a start, we wouldn't know she's a very jealous woman. All we'd see is a good singer and a man who obviously fancies her. Of course, if you leave the scenes as they are, you intrigue the audience by what you've left out. What happened between scenes 1 and 2? Why is Carl blowing her a kiss after she hit his new lover? Why did he then walk out? It opens up a lot of possibilities for the writer to explore.

Exploration is the key to writing a step outline. Many writers write their step outlines on index cards and move them about until they get the 'shape' they want. Experiment to find a method that works for you, but remember – your characters should drive the plot, so show how they develop and grow.

INTRODUCING A SUBPLOT

Now is the time to think about your subplot. A good subplot should add depth to your main plot and main character; it should relate to main story line and show an added dimension to the main character. The subplot allows us to see the personal lives of our characters: their hopes, fears and flaws. The subplot is where your character changes. Once you know the big emotional conflict which your protagonist will be forced to resolve, or the theme of your screenplay, you can create subplots which illustrate different aspects and potential outcomes. That way you will be digging deeper into the story, rather than grafting on unrelated subplots from the outside.

Remember this when you're writing your step outline.

WHAT IS A SYNOPSIS? *SUMMARY – Selling tool*

A synopsis is often confused with an outline because it is also a summary of your story. But a synopsis is a selling tool, and as such it should be concise and intriguing enough to get an agent or producer eager to read your script. I always edit my synopses down to one page as busy people have little time. *(1 page)*

Make sure when writing your synopsis that the 'hero' (protagonist), and 'villain' (antagonist) are clearly defined. Briefly, show how the plot develops, how it complicates and how it's resolved. To write a good synopsis *you* need to know how your story ends (see below).

> **N.B.** *What is very important when writing a synopsis is to reflect the genre you're writing for. For example, if you're writing a thriller your synopsis should be edgy, exciting and intriguing, if you're writing a horror, it should make a reader's flesh creep, and if you're writing a comedy it should make them smile a few times, or better still laugh.*

The decision whether to tell the reader everything in a synopsis if you're writing a mystery or thriller is a tricky one. Some film companies (and agents) like to know exactly how the script ends and don't want any secrets. If your story has a brilliant plot twist or surprise ending like *Sixth Sense* this can be a major selling point for your project and you shouldn't throw away the chance to impress people by not telling them this great ending.

However, many people think that a synopsis should intrigue the reader without necessarily telling them everything. The only way to find out exactly what people want is to ring them up with a brilliant pitch (see Chapter 14) and ask them.

Whether you reveal the ending or not, your synopsis should be an exciting read; it should convey your passion for your story and make the reader feel that they must read the script.

> Remember, a synopsis must be brief and dynamic enough to appeal to a film producer because he or she is the one who ultimately has to raise the funds for the film.

SAMPLE SYNOPSIS

In the synopsis of my screenplay *The Day of the Swans* below, you will see that I haven't explained exactly what is going to happen to my main character at the end. What I have done is to introduce my major characters, briefly explain their relationships, shown conflict and given the outline of the story. Anna (my protagonist) is a clinical psychologist with a stable, happy life, but we know she's going to have problems the moment Stefan starts stalking her. The fact that she's pregnant increases the tension and makes us worry that something awful is going to happen to her.

THE DAY OF THE SWANS

ANNA NASH is a beautiful, trainee clinical psychologist who seems to have everything: a happy marriage to her husband TIM and the devoted love of her parents CELIA and PAUL BAKER. Then one day an Austrian client called STEFAN walks into the clinic where Anna works and her stable world starts to disintegrate.

She's disturbed to find herself attracted to him, especially as she discovers she's pregnant. Stefan intrigues her with fragments of his past and intimates that she is part of it. Soon her dreams are full of these memories and the line between reality and fiction becomes blurred. Stefan explains that they were separated when she was three and she was adopted: she's the sister he's been searching for,

for years. Anna thinks that she's dealing with a man with a delusional personality disorder and discusses his case with MAX PARIS, her supervisor and friend. Max asks her if she wants him to treat Stefan, but Anna knows she must prove capable of being a good psychologist.

After each session with Anna, Stefan goes home to work on an imaginative painting of a 13-year-old boy and a small girl running along a beautiful coastline. Overhead, swans fly.

Anna's normally deep sleep is disturbed by a recurring dream: two children are running along a coastline. Overhead, a flock of swans fly in a V-formation. She tells Tim she's exhausted and they decide to go on holiday; but Anna is adamant – she only wants to go to Wales. Tim is amazed because Anna's never mentioned Wales before. They go to a spectacular place on the Welsh coast and start to enjoy themselves until they take a tour of some caves. Anna sees Stefan there and nearly faints.

Once back in the hotel, Anna tells Tim that one of her clients is stalking her. Tim is horrified and wants to call the police, but Anna stops him and doesn't know why.

When they get home, she questions her parents about her early childhood and when their answers are evasive, she feels that her stable world is falling apart. Anna eventually discovers she was adopted.

In her adoption file, she unearths a traumatic past: 25 years earlier her father fell from a cliff and her mother was put in a psychiatric hospital. She discovers which clinic her birth mother, RENATE, is living in and goes to see her. Anna is appalled when she tells her that Stefan killed someone.

Anna rushes from the clinic to find Stefan waiting outside. He comforts her by telling her that Renate lives in a world of fiction – Anna mustn't believe a word she says. Stefan says he'll drive her home, but turns instead onto the M25 and drives towards a beautiful white house on a cliff in Wales.

Max becomes increasingly concerned about Anna and goes to the social services. He discovers something odd about Anna's file and checks old newspapers on the Internet.

In the meantime, Anna's parents have broken into Stefan's house to discover numerous photos of baby Anna standing outside a white house with a woman who's exactly like her. But when they look closer, they realize that the woman really *is* Anna. The photos are fakes. When they show Max the photo, he knows that's where Stefan has taken her – to the place where his hated father died. Max knows it is vital they reach her before Stefan 'remembers' that Anna really isn't his sister after all.

> **N.B.** *Note that every time I introduce a new character I use capital letters. This is a screen convention which highlights the number of characters in the script. More script conventions are given in Chapter 11.*

WHAT IS A TREATMENT?

A treatment is similar to an outline, but can run from two to twenty pages (sometimes even longer in the States). Like an outline, it is a blueprint for a screenplay.

The treatment should reveal the full structure of the story by showing the personalities of the major and minor characters, their relationships, and how they change and develop. Some producers never want to see a treatment, only an exciting synopsis, but be prepared for others to ask for one, so have it ready. When writing a treatment make sure it's dramatic, concise and visual. Like the outline, it should read like an exciting short story.

Writing a treatment

1. It is written in either 12-point Courier or 12-point Times New Roman in the present tense.

2. Don't use dialogue, unless you have some great dialogue that sums up a character in a few lines.

3. Explain where and when the story takes place (location and period).

4. Be clear about whose point of view the story is written from.

5. Show the key dramatic Turning Points.

6. Always use active verbs, i.e. 'John walks'...not 'John was walking'.

7. Don't use elaborate metaphors or pages of exposition. You're not writing a book.

8. Use the length of your script as a guide to the length of your treatment. For example, if your script is 100 pages, make your treatment 10 pages long.

9. Tell the reader why people will want to watch your film at the end of the treatment. Tell the reader what market you wrote your script for, i.e. do some research into your genre. Your professionalism will impress people.

Remember a strong script is based on strong structure. It's like building an amazingly original house. Get the foundations right and you can build in any direction you want.

EXERCISE

1. Write an outline for your script.
2. Now write a step outline from your outline.

1 hr screenplay 60pp 60 mins
Act 1   15
Act 2 - 30
Act 3   15

3

The Three-Act Structure

STRUCTURING YOUR SCREENPLAY

The three-act structure is popular because it reflects the fundamental nature of storytelling: stories have a beginning, a middle and an end, (although you will see many films that deviate from this structure).

Writing a screenplay can seem an insuperable task without some clear structure, so I'll break it down to make your task much simpler.

Let's assume that you're writing a two-hour (120-page) screenplay.

- ◆ Act I   – 30 pages (approximately 30 minutes).
- ◆ Act II – 60 pages (approximately 60 minutes).
- ◆ Act III – 30 pages (approximately 30 minutes).

These page counts are obviously approximate, but the time-tested three-act breakdown will keep you from running out of story. You might think that this structure is formulaic, but it's important to have a tight structure when you're learning to write screenplays. (Of course, if you're called M. Night Shyamalan, you can create your own rules, but until you have that power, learn the tried and tested ones first.)

We are going to look at the 1985 film *Witness* with Harrison Ford to illustrate this structure so you will need the script to hand. (Log onto *www.simplyscripts.com* and download a copy.)

ACT I – THE SET UP

In the opening scenes of your screenplay it is vitally important to 'hook' the audience and to ensure that they know exactly what genre of film they're watching.

One of the most powerful ways to open a screenplay is with an image. Visualization gives us a strong sense of the place, mood, texture and often the theme.

Notice how *Witness* starts:

- grain blowing in the wind;
- Amish people dressed in traditional black, walking through the grain;
- Amish wagons moving to the sound of a horse;
- a farmhouse;
- a funeral;
- faces.

The slow lyrical pace reflects the rhythm of Amish community. (This tranquillity will clash violently with John Book's life as an American cop.)

The story

See Robbie + Isla   Holy war

After the image, begins the story. We need to see any important characters who will be part of the plot. We need to know where we are, what is going on. Then we need the inciting incident or catalyst to push the script forward.

The inciting incident

In *Witness*, the inciting incident is a murder in a toilet. A small Amish boy called Samuel is the only witness. He knows that two men were present, but he only sees one face. It's at this point that we meet tough American cop John Book (Harrison Ford). He's in charge of the case – he has the problem of finding the murderer (his goal).

Act I should focus on the main character/s and his/their problem. We discover that Book is insensitive, ambitious and uses people. Yet he has to work with an Amish woman and her sensitive child who care about people and hate violence. Hence, we have an immediate clash between two conflicting worlds.

First Turning Point
Act I of *Witness*:

◆ Samuel, a young Amish boy witnesses a murder, which leads to –

◆ Samuel and Rachel, his widowed mother, meeting tough cop John Book. They are appalled by Book's violent methods. Book insists that Samuel goes to police headquarters, which leads to –

◆ Samuel identifying Book's colleague McFee, which leads to –

◆ First Turning Point – McFee trying to kill John, but only wounding him. This Turning Point leads into the second act where John disappears with Rachel and Samuel.

The first Turning Point in *Witness* is 32 minutes into the story. After John explains to his boss Schaeffer that a witness has given positive ID on Mcfee (only these two men know this), Book is ambushed in his garage. This opens up all sorts of corruption within the police as Brook realizes Schaeffer is in on the crime.

This raises the stakes dramatically and pushes the film in a new direction.

In fact, we can sum up Act I of *Witness* like this:

Problem:	A murder
Goal:	To catch killer
Action:	Book investigates the murder
Crisis:	Book discovers a fellow cop is involved
Turning Point:	The shoot-out scene in garage which forces Book into hiding

Basically, a Turning Point, (TP) is some sort of catalyst which spins the action into a dramatic new direction, raises the stakes and is often a moment of decision on the part of the main character.

ACT II – COMPLICATING THE CONFLICT

In Act II you must complicate your story's conflict by showing that the problem facing the protagonist is more far-reaching than he supposed. If he doesn't adapt, he won't survive.

After your first Turning Point, we must see your character react to it. After John is wounded, he's very concerned about Rachel and Samuel, so he drives them back to the Amish community to protect them. This leads to John collapsing from his wound and having to stay in the Amish community. (The beginning of the subplot is the growing relationship between John and Rachel.) He is nursed by Rachel and realizes that the values of the Amish community are attractive – so attractive that Book helps to build a barn in an overlong scene. (Apparently, before Harrison Ford became an actor he was a carpenter and he loved the barn-building sequence so much he wouldn't let any part of it be edited!)

Transforming the characters

It is in Act II that we see the beginning of Book's gradual character transformation through his love for Rachel. In fact, 45 minutes into the film, he gives her his gun (the tough cop in Act I would never have done this), even though he knows Schaeffer and McFee are looking for him. This simple action integrates the subplot with the main plot (finding a killer). It also shows that the solution to Book's problem doesn't lie in a gun but in his need to change from being an aggressive cop who thinks only of himself into a more likeable human being. We see the romantic side to Book when he tries to teach Rachel to dance in a barn and almost kisses her.

We also see how Rachel has changed. She obviously found Book crude and was repelled by him in the beginning of the film; she certainly isn't in this scene, in spite of the fact that she is defying all the Amish rules by starting a relationship outside its world and could be forced to leave.

However, the danger within John and Rachel's relationship is magnified tenfold in the main plot: two highly trained killers are looking for John Book. And, of course, he gives them the opportunity to find him at the end of Act II i.e. the second turning point.

The second Turning Point

The second Turning Point occurs when John goes to the nearest town with other Amish people, dressed like them. But when the Amish men are taunted by some of the locals, John beats them up (which a real Amish person would never do).

We can see from his reaction that Book now obviously respects the Amish people enough to stand up for them, even if they won't. However, because of his reaction, John's cover is blown. He is seen by someone and the information is given to Mcfee and Schaeffer. They go after him and so we are thrown into Act III.

ACT III – INTENSIFYING THE ACTION

This act should have the fastest pacing of all the acts. Incidents should be happening swiftly and lead inexorably to the climax.

This is where you bring in as many conflicts for your character to face as possible. It must seem impossible for him to succeed because of these problems and his character flaws. It was a mistake for Book not to involve other cops when he discovered that Schaeffer was corrupt, but Book was arrogant enough to believe he could sort out the corruption within the police force by himself. (This arrogance gets his partner killed.)

However, because we have seen the softer side of John in the Amish community, we are now on his side. He has allowed himself to be vulnerable because of Rachel and we want him to succeed. And indeed, Rachel helps him to succeed because she's made him stronger mentally; he now thinks before he acts which helps him outwit his antagonist and boss Schaeffer.

The third act needs to be more intense than the others so that it leads up to the climax.

Climax

The climax occurs about 5–8 pages from the end. If you look at this section in *Witness* you'll see how fast paced it is. The scenes are very short and action-packed with fast intercuts from Book, to the men who want to kill him, to young Samuel ringing the bell to warn the Amish people, to Rachel, now terrified that her son might be killed in cross-fire, back to Book again. There's hardly any dialogue for pages. The climax is incredibly tense and the anticipation that not only will Book be killed, but also young Samuel, makes the suspense very powerful. In front of the whole Amish Community, Book shows that he's stronger than his corrupt boss by outwitting Schaeffer.

After the climax, the pace should slow so that the tension can be released. In *Witness*, we see Book and Rachel separating – their differing lifestyles can't be overcome. The last scene focuses on an Amish man who loves Rachel and hints at where Rachel's future lies.

> Remember when you're writing your script: create a strong, visual style with credible, exciting complications to fascinate your audience.

> **N.B.** *Many films don't use this structure and yet still work. However, if you try to copy films like Tootsie (which many people think has five acts) or Memento which uses flashbacks and flashforwards to confuse or intrigue the audience (depending on whether you like or hate the film), you'll find your plot meandering all over the place. As I said before, learn proven screenwriting structure before you try to break it.*

EXERCISE

Look at your step outline again in the light of this chapter. Have you got a tight structure? If not, rework the outline.

4

The Inciting Incident

WHAT IS AN INCITING INCIDENT?

This is an event which gives your main character (your protagonist) a major problem. The rest of the script should show how s/he reacts and overcomes this problem. Remember, you're going to have to write between 100 and 120 pages, so make the inciting incident big enough to force your protagonist to react strongly.

In this chapter we look at some examples. Here is the first:

Your hero Daniel is at a dinner party. There's an empty chair beside him and everyone asks him where his girlfriend Emma is. He doesn't know and looks worried. The telephone rings and the hostess answers it. She looks shocked as she listens and tells Daniel that Emma has just been arrested by the police after a great deal of money was discovered in her car. They are now on their way to question him. Dan is stunned, but we see from everyone's reaction that they think Daniel is implicated.

This scenario forces us to ask questions. Where did the money come from? How did it get into Emma's car? Why has Emma been arrested so quickly? Are Daniel's 'friends' correct in suspecting that he is involved? What is he going to do now?

HOOKING THE AUDIENCE

As writers, we need to make the inciting incident powerful enough to hook the audience. One way to do this is make the audience identity with your hero/heroine *before* the inciting incident, i.e. make them care about what happens to Daniel and Emma. If you don't care about your main characters, why should the audience follow their story?

To demonstrate how you could do this, let's start the scenario above with another scene. This time we open with Daniel and Emma having a wonderful time on an exotic island. I'd use a series of shots to show how happy they are without any dialogue. Then I'd finish this scene with some dialogue: Daniel proposes and Emma accepts. Then I'd cut straight to the dinner party scene.

Now the audience will be far more curious by Emma's absence and will be more involved with both characters. By cutting from a proposal scene to a dinner party the audience will be curious to know what exactly happened between scenes 1 and 2. Has Emma done something illegal? Is Daniel involved? Or have they both been framed and, if so, how are they going to clear themselves? We are worried for them because we saw how happy they were in the first scene.

This is a simple but effective technique for involving your audience at the beginning of your script.

Here's another scenario:

Susanna, your heroine, has to have a DNA test (You decide why – make it powerful.) She's appalled to discover that her beloved father isn't related to her at all. Her life is turned upside down as she's always felt secure knowing that her parents are devoted to her and each other. She now feels angry and betrayed by her mother and goes on a quest to discover her true background. (If this was a thriller, you could make your heroine's quest a roller coaster of false leads, recriminations and shocking discoveries which force her to confront her mother in a powerful climactic scene.)

But you have to make us care about Susanna's journey of discovery. One way to involve us would be to have flashbacks to scenes of Susanna's idyllic childhood with her parents. Once we see how happy the three of them are, we want to know what happened to make Susanna's mother have a child with another man.

EXERCISE

Write an inciting incident for your screenplay.

Remember to show the incident in the most visual way you can. Use the minimum of dialogue and try to move the story forward by using character actions and reactions.

(5) Writing Powerful Opening Scenes

Where are you going to start your story (your point of entry)? The opening of any screenplay must have a great 'hook' to ensure that the reader continues reading. Most script readers won't read beyond the first ten pages if they're bored or confused so make sure they aren't!

Let's look at how you could open a screenplay in a variety of genres using a number of techniques.

A SCI-FI OPENING

```
FADE IN
COMPUTER SCREEN
So close it has no boundaries.

A blinking cursor pulses in the electric darkness
like a heart coursing with phosphorous light,
burning beneath the derma of black-neon glass.

A phone BEGINS to ring LOUDLY. The cursor continues
to throb until -

                    MAN (V.O.)
          Hello?
```

Data now slashes across the screen too fast to read.

```
                    SCREEN
            Call trans opt: received. 2-19-96 13-24-
            18. REC: Log...
                    WOMAN (V.O.)
            I'm inside. Anything to report?
```

This opening comes from the *Matrix* which was written by Larry and Andy Wachowski. Can you see how it introduces the genre of sci-fi immediately? We're thrown into a strange computer world. (In fact, this one simple close up of a computer foreshadows the whole of the *Matrix* story very cleverly.) We're disorientated because the writer only allows us to see the computer screen; we only hear the voices of humans in voice over (V.O.).

The description we read also echoes this strange world and sets up the dark edgy mood of the film. Couple this with the sparse dialogue and the audience is left asking multiple questions. Where are we? What period of time are we in? Who's the man? Who's the woman? What's she inside? We later find out that the man is called Cypher and the woman Trinity. Even the names reflect the strangeness of this world. If you want mystery, create an opening like this, but be careful not to annoy the reader by being too obscure. (You can do that when you're famous!)

A FANTASY OPENING

FADE IN

EXT. A STEEP LUSH GREEN HILL - DAY

The hill is covered with exquisite flowers and
trees. This is a beautiful place.

JACK and JILL (15) walk hand in hand up a hill
carrying a large bucket between them. They smile at
each other.

> VOICE (O.S)
> Jack and Jill walk up the
> hill to fetch a pail of
> water. But Jack doesn't fall
> down... he -

Jack and Jill stare down at the bucket.

THEIR POV. The bucket is full of water which shimmers
to reveal a strange world full of surreal sights.

> VOICE (O.S)
> looks down into a new world...

EXT. AN ANIMATED BLUE HILL - DAY

Jack and Jill (now animated figures) climb up a
multi-coloured hill towards a strange looking well.
They look very nervous.

> VOICE (O.S)
> And suddenly they're inside the world and we
> know that something awful is going to
> happen to them.

In this short extract, I've created suspense by moving from a beautiful 'real' world into one of animated fantasy in which anything can happen. The audience will obviously want to know what's going to happen next.

There are many innovative ways of opening a fantasy film. Terry Rossio and Ted Elliot open *Shrek* with a stream of light cutting through darkness to illuminate an old book. The book opens to reveal a picture of a Princess running through a field with a fairy-tale castle in the background, then a voice over says – 'Once upon a time there was a lovely Princess.'

This inventive opening, (a fairy tale that comments on fairy tales) seduces the reader by making them walk into a magical world. We relax into a world of childhood dreams when we hear those wonderful words 'Once upon a time.'

Notice that in these openings, the speaker is unseen and unidentified. In sci-fi, fantasies and fairy tales, such narration helps draw the audience and reader out of their ordinary world, and into the strange, magical world you're creating. These dialogue passages also create a tone of mystery. (Who is speaking? Where are we?) It intrigues because we know we are going on a strange journey.

AN HISTORICAL DRAMA OPENING

FADE IN:

The PORTRAIT of a STUNNINGLY BEAUTIFUL ENCHANTRESS fills the screen. She's wearing a 1830s white ball-gown with a garland of red flowers in her hair.

INT. 1856. A LECTURE HALL – DAY

RICHARD DAVENPORT, an attractive middle-aged HISTORY LECTURER is standing in front of a group of University students who are staring up at the portrait in awe.

A large sign reads: THE FICTION OF TRUTH. A lecture by Dr. Richard Davenport.

An ELDERLY MAN sits in SHADOWS at the back of the hall.

> RICHARD
>
> I am going to illustrate my lecture today by telling you a story about my journey to Jamaica where I met the woman in the portrait. Yes, this story *is* incredible, but, gentlemen (beat) believe me... everything I am going to tell you is the truth.

FADE UP the ominous SOUND of tribal drums in the background.

> RICHARD
>
> The year was 1831 and I was the same age as you are now.

His eyes sweep around the students' rapt faces.

EXT. 1831. A PLANTATION IN JAMAICA – NIGHT

The SOUND of drums continues.

> RICHARD (VO)
> I met Annie Palmer on her sugar plantation.
> There I saw and experienced things that
> were, at first, beyond my comprehension.

As he speaks A BLACK SLAVE runs terrified across a
field towards the cover of petrified trees in the
forest.

THE SOUND OF THE DRUMS MINGLE WITH THE SOUND OF THE
GALLOPING HOOVES OF A HORSE.

A WHITE HORSE and RIDER charge across the field
towards the slave. The rider, dressed in a white
shirt and black breeches, expertly swings a whip
over his/her head, then lashes it across the slave's
back.

The slave's SCREAMS ECHO through the night.

This is the opening from my script WHITE WITCH. I start the
script with the image; a portrait of one of the main characters in
the film; Annie Palmer, a white witch. The camera then moves out
from the portrait and we realise that we're in a lecture hall. (Note
the use of a date in the scene heading, but no camera directions.)
Here we meet another major character, Richard Davenport, who
is giving a lecture to students called 'The Fiction Of Truth.' (A

small ironic detail which introduces the reader to the idea that 'reality' is often a façade.) I then layer the lecture with the sights and sounds of a Jamaican sugar plantation 30 years earlier. The scenes are shocking and foreshadow the darkness that will follow.

Make every image you use in the opening of your script resonate in the mind of your reader. (And later, the audience in the cinema.)

Anthony Minghella used multi-layering in his script THE ENGLISH PATIENT, (based on the novel by Michael Ondaatje). Africa is a major player in this film. The film opens with a lingering, stunning shot of the contours of the sand in a desert. (Actually shot in Oung Jmel in Tunisia.) Minghella then moves the camera from the shadow of a plane, to the reality of a bi-plane. (Which dates the film for us.) In the plane are the two major characters who are introduced in the script only by the words 'a woman' and 'a man'. Minghella sets up mystery for the reader from the beginning. The multi-layering is intensified by the haunting poignancy of the singing in which the unhappiness between Katherine Clifton [Kristen Scott-Thomas] and Count Almasy [Ralph Fiennes] is foreshadowed. This opening also foreshadows the visual richness of a fascinating film. Down-load a copy of the script from www.simplyscripts.com

The writer Akiva Goldman also uses multi-layering in the opening of A BEAUTIFUL MIND. He starts with a close up of a stained glass window, then pulls back to reveal a reception at Princeton University where we see a large gathering of formally dressed students. One man stands alone, isolated by his lack of interest in the people around him, totally absorbed in studying how the light refracting from his glass paints rainbows on the bar before him.

Each small detail we're shown reveals the nature of the main character: his intelligence [the Princeton setting]; his analytical mind [the geometric shapes he's staring at]; his lack of social skills [he ignores everyone to gaze at the refracting light]. Once again, this opening foreshadows what's to come: here is a character searching for some pattern, some understanding of life, but he's gazing at glass refracting light, rather than being involved with people. This lack of involvement is one of the obstacles he has to overcome during the film; he has to change.

(The early introduction to the hero at the beginning of the screenplay allows the audience to identify with that character.)

A ROMANTIC COMEDY OPENING

FADE IN:

To a painting of VASILISA. A beautiful Russian
Princess from a fairy tale. She's standing in a
forest; her long blonde plait hanging over one
shoulder.

INT. A STUDIO - DAY

A green lacquer box sits on a chair. Vasilisa is
painted on the box. Above her is a Knight on a white
horse.

PULL BACK to - a LARGE CHAOTIC ART STUDIO , full of
blank canvases, mouldy food, ancient furniture,
books, a computer and the lacquer box on an old chair.

A dishevelled artist, DANIEL MADOX (30s) stands in
front of an empty canvas, desperately trying to
squeeze oil paint out of numerous empty tubes. He
throws them on the floor.

His parrot, CHARLIE, watches him from his cage.

> CHARLIE
> A picture paints a thousand words.

> DAN
> At least I can paint. What can you do?

Charlie hops up and down, squawking loudly.

Dan looks everywhere for money. Eventually he finds some loose change and pockets it.

> CHARLIE
> A fool and his money are soon –

> DAN
> Shut up!

Dan covers his cage with a cloth. Charlie attempts a muffled squawk as Dan walks out.

INT. MADAME VOLGA'S HALLWAY – DAY

A dark Victorian hallway. A sign reads: NO PETS ALLOWED.

Dan creeps down the stairs past his Russian landlady's room. MADAME VOLGA opens the door and we hear the faint strains of RUSSIAN SAKHA MUSIC PLAYING. She watches him creeping for a few minutes before shouting out.

> MADAM VOLGA
> Daniel! What for you crawl down the stairs?

> DAN
> Creep, Madam Volga. I'm not crawling.

> MADAM VOLGA
> Creeping. Crawling. It's all the same.
> Your friend Charlie, he is ill? He make
> strange noise.

Dan turns and beams at her.

> DAN
> No, he's just got a sore throat. I was
> creeping because I didn't want to disturb
> you.

> MADAM VOLGA
> You only disturb me when you do not pay the
> money, Daniel.

> DAN
> Ah... the rent. There's a bit of a problem
> there.

> MADAM VOLGA
> Life is always a problem, but we must -

Dan rushes up the stairs.

> DAN
> I've got something for you.

> MADAME VOLGA
> I live in hope.

He rushes down the stairs with a painting and gives it
to Madam Volga. She peers at it. It's full of wild
swirling colours. She shakes her head. She has no
idea what it is.

>   MADAM VOLGA
>   And what is this?

>   DAN
>   Vortex.

>   MADAM
>   So you give me this ... this Vortex instead
>   of money?

>   DAN
>   This painting will be worth a fortune in a
>   hundred years.

>   MADAM
>   I have to wait a hundred years for rent? I'm
>   77 years old, Daniel.

This extract comes from ALCHEMY & ICE, a Romantic Comedy
I've written which centres on the characters of two disparate
young people: Daniel, a penniless artist and Laura, (who we meet
on the next page) an ambitious, but vulnerable young woman who
works in advertising. The opening introduces us to an image from
a fairy tale story. This image will figure strongly throughout the
script as Laura looks exactly like Vasilisa. The image is then
echoed in the small lacquer box on a chair in a studio. This image
is the link between Daniel and Laura who fall chaotically in love.
I have used camera directions here to pull back from the close

shot of the chair to a wide shot of an artist's studio. Here we meet Daniel who has an off-beat life-style, an eccentric parrot and an even more eccentric landlady.

If you're interested in writing Romantic Comedies read as many scripts as you can in this genre and also read Billy Mernit's Book called *Writing The Romantic Comedy.* It's very useful.

A WAR OPENING

```
FADE IN


INT. MIKE'S BEDROOM - NIGHT


MIKE SEYMOUR (30s) is tossing and turning in his
sleep. He's sweating heavily. Suddenly he jerks
upright - wide awake.


He looks around the swaying room in alarm.


He JUMPS out of bed and races for the bathroom in a
blur.


SOUND of Mike throwing up.


ON HIS BEDROOM WALL: NUMEROUS PHOTOS.


1.MIKE (age 10) with his father COLONEL SEYMOUR
(age 48) -


The Colonel is dressed in military uniform. Father
and son stand in the same rigid posture, staring
unsmilingly at the camera. There is a distance
between them.
```

2. MIKE (20s) and COLONEL SEYMOUR (58) -

Mike wears Marine combat gear; his father wears a
Major General's uniform. They stand at Brize Norton
Airfield surrounded by young soldiers going to the
Iraq War. The Major General beams at his son. Mike
smiles back tentatively.

3. MIKE racing across a bullet-riddled street in
Iraq.

4. MIKE (30s) SAM (5) MIKE'S FATHER (68)-

Mike's father (now a civilian) and his grandson Sam
laugh as they fire toy guns at each other. Mike sits
in a chair, watching them morosely.

INT. MIKE'S BATHROOM - NIGHT

Mike washes his ashen face with one hand. On a chair
in the corner is his prosthetic arm.

The opening shot shows us that something has traumatized Mike
so much that he vomits at the memory. Then we are given
numerous visual clues as to what created the trauma. We learn a
lifetime of information about his relationship with his father
through images: we know that he's been coerced into army life
which creates a bond between us and Mike. When we see Mike's
son with his grandfather, we suspect that history is going to repeat
itself and wonder why Mike doesn't stop his son playing at war.
The last short scene shows us the shocking reason: Mike has not
only lost his youthful optimism, but his arm.

> **N.B.** *Note the layout of the description. If you want a reader to notice each small detail, introduce each image on a separate line. It works. (However, be careful you don't overdo this style of layout as your script will run way over 120 pages.)*

PHOTOGRAPHS

Photographs can be used as a shortcut to show your character's back story, but remember to use light and shade when writing a story as dark as this. Don't make every scene traumatic. Remember to lighten tragedy with humour throughout your screenplay, otherwise your audience will leave the cinema feeling very depressed.

Robert Towne uses a photograph to open his brilliant screenplay *Chinatown*. However, this time the photograph fills the whole screen. It's a grainy photo of a couple making love. Towne then layers this visual detail with the sound of a man moaning in anguish. The photo falls and reveals another even more compromising one of the same man and woman in bed. We hear more moans, then a man's voice crying 'Oh no.'

As in the earlier examples, *Chinatown* draws us into the story through an image. Like all great scripts, Towne's opening foreshadows many of the underlying elements that will echo through the film: secrecy, betrayal, sex and surprising revelations. When we realize the moans are not coming from the couple, but from the man viewing the photographs, we begin to see that nothing is what it seems.

N.B. *The script of* Chinatown *is worth studying in detail, not only for its fascinating story line, but for its characterization.*

Using a memorable image

The opening of your screenplay should create the mood and theme so using a memorable image is a great way to start your script. Remember the haunting image at the beginning of *The French Lieutenant's Woman*? Sara Woodruff (Meryl Streep) stands at the quayside of Lyme Regis, staring out into a turbulent sea. She turns in slow motion towards the camera and Charles Smithson (Jeremy Irons) is mesmerized by her face framed by the green hood of her long cloak. That's how powerful images can be (so powerful that they used this image in a poster to advertise the film).

EXERCISE

1. Create a powerful image to establish the genre of your film.
2. Now write the first two scenes.

6

Writing Compelling Scenes

'STARTING LATE, LEAVING EARLY'

I'm sure you've heard the expression 'start late, leave early' when writing scenes. But what does this actually mean? Let's take the following scenario as an example.

> A husband (Martin) and wife (Stella) are separated. They arrange to meet for dinner to talk about their future and you decide that Stella is going to tell him she wants a divorce. The main point of this scene is that Stella wants a divorce. (There *must* be a point to every scene.) So, we don't linger over details like letting them choose what they are going to wear, their journey to the restaurant or their small talk when they meet, unless *one or more of these small details are vitally important later in the script.* Let's start the scene in a lively restaurant where people are enjoying themselves – except for our couple who eat in silence. We can see from their body language that there's tension. Stella puts down her cutlery and says bluntly: 'I want a divorce.'

This is a powerful way to end the scene. That's the only line of dialogue between two people surrounded by other people enjoying themselves. (A contrasting background to your main characters' situation always makes them stand out.)

However, here's another way in which you can create tension and anticipation in an audience – show them in a short scene before they meet in the restaurant. This time you show Martin getting ready in his bedroom. He opens a drawer, brings out a hypodermic syringe, tests it, smiles and puts it back in the drawer.

You have now done two things: pushed your story forward and created anticipation in your audience. What's he going to do with the syringe? Why does he smile?

This curiosity is heightened when you cut to the scene in a lively, upmarket restaurant. Here we meet Stella, who's waiting for him. She tenses as he walks towards her. Neither of them smile. He just sits down and looks at the menu. Stella looks at him.

All this non-verbal interaction gives the audience clues about their failing relationship so we're not surprised this time when she says 'I want a divorce.' But we would be if Martin's reaction was to ask her back for a glass of champagne – to celebrate their divorce. We know that Martin is going to use the syringe on Stella and we will be full of worried anticipation.

TRANSITIONS

'Transitions' link one scene to the next, like a bridge. The way you leave one scene and enter another is important. You have to pay attention to the unwritten space between your scenes.

Remember, you can't show all that is happening within the timescale of the film. i.e. time will elapse between scenes, but you must know exactly what your characters are doing during these times. By not filling in all the blanks for the audience and giving them less, the audience will be more engaged.

In real life, we open our eyes, get out of bed, put on clothes, go downstairs, etc. But these shots are too literal and boring. Unless these details are significant to your story, i.e. you want to make the audience wait to find out what the character discovers downstairs.)

CHOICES

The art of cinematic storytelling often comes from the choices we make about *what we leave out of the scene*; the meanings we create by connecting scenes that don't happen in a continuous flow. For example, Frances opens her eyes in bed, then in the next scene, she's sitting at her desk, hard at work. The meaning created via those two linked scenes might be: every waking moment of Frances' life is about work. The link between scenes now has some significance and that's a key function of transitions: maintaining logic as we leap through time and space. Treat the audience with respect and allow them to work out parts of the story on their own.

Remember the scene in *Tootsie* when difficult actor Michael (Dustin Hoffman) is told by his agent that no one wants to work with him? Michael shouts confrontationally. 'Oh, yeah!' In the next scene we see Michael in drag walking down the street. It's a great transition. It tells the audience that Michael is determined to prove his agent wrong, even if the only way he can do it is to 'become' a woman, and it's also funny.

> Remember, pacing can be increased by shortening the amount of time we spend in the scene after the vital nugget of information has been given.

SCREEN ACTION

Screen action is also called description. It's the action that takes place on the screen and should be written visually. The important word here is *visual*.

'Show, don't tell', is perhaps, the oldest axiom in the dramatic writing world, but it's amazing how many screenwriters still don't remember it. The 'visual' is paramount in screenwriting. For example, if a character is claustrophobic, don't let your character tell us he's claustrophobic. Put him in a lift or a pothole (anywhere that's confined) and let's see his reaction. This is far more powerful as it forces us to engage in the story. *We become concerned with a character's plight through visuals, not by being told.*

In view of this, I'm sure you can see what's wrong with this description/action.

```
EXT. MARK'S GARDEN - DAY


Mark, a successful landscape gardener, walks into
the garden, thinking about his children. Two boys
suddenly run into the garden.
```

It's not visual, is it? We aren't showing that Mark is (a) successful, (b) he's a landscape gardener, (c) what his garden looks like (d) what he's thinking, (e) what his personality is like.

Let's rewrite the above, to make it visual and show you his personality

```
EXT. MARK'S GARDEN - DAY


The garden is a designer's dream: ornamental arches
trail numerous colourful flowers, winding pebbled
pathways lead to exotic plants and pagodas. High in
an ancient oak tree, is a stunning tree house.


MARK (attractive, early 40s), wearing casual but
expensive clothes, strolls into the garden, dead-
heads one flower and smiles as his two boys (7 and 9)
race down the garden towards the tree house. He
rushes after them and play-fights with them to climb
up first. They squeal with laughter.
```

Now we can visualize the garden, see that Mark is successful and relaxed: he 'strolls' into his stunning garden and has expensive clothes, happy children and a great relationship with them. However, his gesture of dead-heading a flower shows a small detail about why he's successful: he's also meticulous. All these details give the audience visual clues about Mark's life without a word of dialogue being spoken.

Every moment in a screenplay takes place now. So avoid any time constructions, such as clauses that use the words like 'while', 'before', 'after', 'when' or 'then'.

Don't try to make your information/action sound literary. Writing great screenplays is a skill in devising precise, visual details.

However, these details don't have to be boring. Think laterally about giving the reader interesting, concise information about each character like:

    Darryl comes trotting down the stairs. Polyester was
    made for this man. (From Carrie Kourie's *Thelma and
    Louise*.)

We don't know whether Darryl is short or tall, fat or thin, attractive or ugly – or even what he is wearing. But we still know exactly what Darryl is like. This is an instant snapshot of a character. He's got no style, 'polyester was made' for him. He comes 'trotting' down the stairs. What alpha male 'trots'?

> **N.B.** *When writing your scenes, always think how to make it visual and how to reveal aspects of your character's personality. Use visual sentences that put pictures in the reader's mind.*

Remember, try to write the script so the reader can read it at the same pace as an audience would see it.

GROUP SCENES

When you are writing a group scene, think how to make it interesting. E.g. you have a clash between a local hunt and an anti-blood sports faction. Where will you have the clash? Make it dramatic. How about outside the Master of the Hunt's palatial house? We see the protesters knocking out the alarm system on the gates, then standing in front of them. However, make sure you don't depict all 'hunters' as generic Hooray Henrys or the anti-blood sports brigade as angry, scruffy young men.

Make us involved with the scene by placing a few surprising people in each 'camp'. Among the protesters could be a young mother carrying a baby. As the protesters all join hands to form a human chain so that the hunt can't get past them, the young mother looks down at her sleeping baby, snug in his baby carrier on her stomach, and touches his head gently. Immediately, the audience becomes involved because the writer has made the protest personal; a mother is so passionate about her beliefs that she's brought her baby with her, but we worry that the baby will be hurt.

You then cut to the jovial gathering of red-coated men and woman on horses, waiting for the Master of the Hunt to mount, completely unaware of the protestors waiting at the bottom of the drive. Everyone is full of excited anticipation – everyone except a nervous teenage boy on a skittish horse being glared at by his suddenly iron-faced father, the Master of the Hunt. It's obvious the boy is a reluctant hunter.

Each small detail involves the reader far more than if you had written:

    A group of protestors form a human chain as they wait
    for the local hunt to ride up to them.

DETAILS

Make every detail count by giving the reader of the script powerful visual images. What's the weather like? Is there a storm approaching or is it a blisteringly hot day? The weather could also play a part in the scene. For example, the woman (or the teenager) could feel faint in the heat. How would this impact on the resulting clash between the two groups?

What sounds are important in the scene? The barking of dogs? People laughing outside the house? You could contrast these sounds with the silence of the waiting protestors. Or make the baby wake up and start crying just as the hunt rides towards the protestors. People always become involved when you make something personal.

STUDYING EXAMPLES

Watch the film *To Kill a Mocking Bird* (1962) and study the lynch mob scene. The mob is determined to kill a black man accused of raping a white woman. Yet look how one little girl, nicknamed 'Scout', changes a mob of men into embarrassed individuals. She innocently picks out the father of a friend of hers in the crowd and says: 'Don't you remember me, Mr Cunningham...I go to school with your boy. Walter is a nice boy. Tell him hey from me, won't you?' Mr Cunningham is now no longer part of a group but a father, an individual with responsibilities. He slinks away, ashamed of what he was going to do.

Or take the harrowing scene in *Sophie's Choice* (1982) when Sophie (Meryl Streep) is told to choose which of her children should be killed in a concentration camp. The scene changes from the general chaos of the camp and becomes intensely personal when we see the look of profound anguish on her face as she whispers. 'Don't ask me to choose.' Of course, she's forced to and we are appalled by the screams of her little girl as she is hauled away to be killed.

COMPELLING SCENES

Every time you write a scene ask yourself these questions:

1. Who needs to be in this scene? Why?

2. Why do I need to set this scene in this location?

3. What's the most surprising thing that could happen in this scene? (Think laterally.)

4. Is this scene moving my story forward?

5. Am I showing the audience what motivates my characters and how they feel? (Show this through their body language and actions. i.e. externalize how your characters feel so we can see it, without the use of dialogue.)

6. What symbols am I using to show the inner life of my main character/s? For example, a crucifix on your protagonist's bedroom wall tells us volumes about his/her beliefs without a word of dialogue being spoken. (The recurring symbol that sums up John Book's life, in Act I of *Witness*, is a gun.)

7. What is the essential action you need for each scene?

8. What is the minimum information you need us to know for the scene to make sense and be credible?

9. What would happen if you begin the scene later?

10. Similarly, what would happen if the scene ends earlier?

VARIATION

Most scenes are around a quarter of a page to four pages long, but you can afford to have a few longer scenes. (In fact, *Good Will Hunting* has one scene with Robin Williams speaking for over four pages, but this is very unusual.) It's vitally important to vary the pace and rhythm of your scenes. For example, if you're writing a thriller, allow the audience time to relax a little before you ratchet up the suspense again. An invaluable way to get a feel for whether your scenes and dialogue are working is to have the script read aloud by actors. (The London Screenwriters' Workshop runs script-reading meetings with professional actors.) Or you could approach your local amateur group who are often happy to read scripts in front of an invited audience.

Remember: if you visualize your locations, your characters and their actions, you will engage the script reader and s/he will be far more likely to pass your script up the line towards production.

EXERCISE

Write three more scenes from your step outline, using all the points you've learned in this chapter.

7

Techniques to Make Your Script Stand Out

AVOID CAMERA DIRECTIONS

Use the minimum of camera directions in your script. It destroys the reader's attempt to imagine the film in his or her own head and annoys the director. He feels you're telling him what to do. In other words, don't write:

```
CLOSEUP OF FEET walking along the floor. We TRACK
ALONG WITH the feet until they disappear...
```

Write:

```
FEET walk across the floor and disappear behind a
door...
```

The reader now only 'sees' what the writer wants him or her to see and is not pushed out of the story.

Below are more examples of how to write your own 'camera directions' without anyone being aware of them.

You want to open your script with a close up of an eye. (If you do, make sure that eyes have significance later in the script.)

With camera directions:

```
C.U. of a large eye.
```

Without camera directions:

```
A LARGE BLUE EYE fills the screen.
```

I've used capital letters so that this important visual detail stands out (and I've added colour). This version is far more visual and I'm not pulling the reader out of the story.

With camera directions:

```
C.U. of SONIA WILSON (30s), an attractive blonde,
walking. PULL BACK to a large sitting room. She sits
down in a chair and shudders.
```

Without camera directions:

```
WHITE HIGH-HEELED SHOES, half covered in blood, tap
over a parquet floor.
```

```
SONIA WILSON (30s) an attractive blonde, leans
against the bar in a large sitting room, pours
herself a large glass of whisky and downs it in one.
```

This latter version is more intriguing because I've used visual and auditory detail:

1. Sound – two white shoes tap across a parquet floor. (No sound at all if she walked over a carpet);

2.   Sight – the contrast between white shoes and red blood;

3.   Action – I've also established that whatever has happened has shocked Sonia because she knocks back a lot of whisky.

Each small detail strengthens the scene: we want to know what's happened in the past and what's going to happen in the future. So remember, make every detail you use in a scene have significance. Don't be vague.

With camera directions:

```
CLOSE on a quill moving on parchment.
```

Without camera directions:

```
A quill scratches over parchment.
```

I've now added a small sound.

With camera directions:

```
C.U. SAMUEL (50s), a haggard man, writes in a diary at
an expensive desk. CLOSE on a photograph of his
family. CLOSE on Samuel's distraught face. ANGLE on
his diary. We see the words. 'I LOVE YOU' as Samuel
writes in it. PULL BACK to reveal a rope hanging from
a beam in the study.
```

Without camera directions:

```
SAMUEL, 50s, haggard, is hunched over his expensive
```

```
desk, writing. His face is distraught as he looks at a
photograph of his family. He writes I LOVE YOU in his
diary.


A LARGE ROPE hangs from a beam, waiting...
```

This second version directs the camera to look at different things in the scene, but does so subtly. Also note the shocking image of the rope on a separate line which makes the image stand out for the reader. And the small addition of the word 'waiting' creates foreboding. (The image of the rope is an example of foreshadowing which we look at next.)

FORESHADOWING

This is a simple, but powerful technique which you should think about before you begin writing the script. It means planting small visual clues as to what is going to happen later. (Put them in your step outline.)

Examples

Audiences like to see foreshadowing because it allows them some input into the film: they like to try to work out what's going to happen next. Films like *Psycho*, *Sixth Sense* and *The Others* use foreshadowing to great effect to keep the audience hooked and, of course, all have great twists at the end.

Look at how Hitchcock uses foreshadowing in *Psycho* by showing Norman Bates' (Anthony Perkins) interest in preserving things (his grotesque stuffed birds) and then later, linking this interest to the presence of his mother's desiccated remains in the cellar. This final twist is a typical Hitchcockian technique. Up to this moment, the audience has been led to believe that Norman's unseen mother is alive. She must be alive because we hear her voice off camera! (I don't know if you've noticed, but this amazing twist is also used by M. Night Shyamalan in his film *Sixth Sense*.)

In *Sixth Sense*, there are scenes which (apparently) show a lack of communication between Malcolm and Anna Crowe; there are scenes which show Malcolm's (apparent) alienation from the world. It is only at the end of the script that we discover that Malcolm is really dead. Shyamalan, like Hitchcock, has cleverly used foreshadowing to lead the audience to make false conclusions.

> Remember: think carefully about planting small subtle clues to keep your audience hooked and where your twists and turns will occur.

USING SUBTEXT

Subtext is always implied, never explicit. It is revealed in the unspoken thoughts and motives of your characters, i.e. what they really think and believe. What you leave out of a scene is its subtext. Pushing this just beneath the surface of the dialogue is what makes scenes so interesting for us because we are forced to discover things for ourselves.

There is a lot of subtext in the above scene with Samuel.

1. We know that he loves his family.

2. We know that something awful must have happened to him.

3. We know he's going to commit suicide in spite of that love.

Many writers use subtext to great effect in their screenplays. For example, Mario Puzo uses it to show the changing character of Michael Corleone in *The Godfather*. (1972) We see him gradually change from the all-American hero to a mobster. Puzo (and, of course, Al Pacino who plays Michael brilliantly) wanted this character to show these changes subtly through his facial expressions and clipped dialogue.

When Don Corleone is shot, Michael is Christmas shopping with his American girlfriend. We see him pause in stunned disbelief as he discovers the news on the crowded streets of New York. The next scene cuts immediately to the Don's office which is full of his henchmen and his sons. Michael's face has already visibly changed from the boyish naivety of the opening earlier scenes to a pensive, calculating expression and his body language is now more restrained. He sits quietly to the side, studying the men, who are trained killers. His eyes are shrewder, more watchful. The idealistic young man is disappearing. When he finally speaks, his dialogue has already been subtly foreshadowed: he tells them he is going to kill the culprits. The men are initially stunned – this is idealistic Mike, but once they see his expression and hear him say to his brother 'it's not personal, Sonny, it's business,' they know he's become one of them. (And so do we.) The way Michael's personality changes is summed up by his chilling words: 'Keep your friends close, but your enemies closer.' You wouldn't want to mess with a character who thinks like this.

The film *American Beauty* (1999) is full of subtext and well worth studying too. On the surface, it's a film about Lester, a middle-aged man going through mid life crisis, but the subtext shows us how Lester gradually learns to love himself; it also shows us that an acceptance of death can be beautiful.

ADVERBS

Adverbs are called 'parentheticals' in screenplays and are used to convey a character's emotional state, e.g. 'angrily', 'sincerely', 'coyly', etc. However, the character's emotional state should be clear from your plot and dialogue, so use parentheticals very sparingly.

Here are a few reasons to use parentheses within dialogue:

1. To clarify to whom a person is speaking if there're more than two people in the room, i.e. (to Maria).

2. If it's important for us to know how a person is speaking, i.e. 'whispering'.

3. If the character really means the opposite of what they're saying, e.g.

```
                    EMMA
                (playfully)
        You bastard.
```

Ask yourself why you need to use words like 'angrily', 'plaintively', 'slyly', 'happily'. Are you adding detail, or avoiding it? Avoiding adverbs helps you hone your writing skills; it forces you to think of ways to present information in a creative way. Look at the following:

With adverb:

```
Craig beats Wayne violently with a crowbar.
```

It's difficult to beat someone without violence, isn't it? Yet, in spite of the adverb, the information is bland because it tells the reader little about the action within the scene.

Without the adverb:

    Bone shatters, blood sprays across Craig's body as
    he smashes the crowbar down onto Wayne's head. He
    smiles.

Now the reader knows two things: (1) exactly how Craig beats Wayne, i.e. the scene is now visual, and (2) that he enjoys doing it. That smile is sinister.

THE OVERUSE OF 'WE'

There is no need to say 'we' see or hear anything. Don't tell the reader what they're seeing, show them; don't tell them what they're hearing, give them the sound.

With:

    We see an angry BABOON rattling the bars of his cage.
    We hear a distant SCREAM. We see the baboon
    listening.

Without:

    An angry BABOON rattles the bars of his cage. A
    distant SCREAM. The baboon listens.

The simple omission of 'we' makes the script tighter and easier to read.

Go through your work to excise all these little additions and rewrite the descriptions so they are stronger and more concise.

TO BE OR NOT TO BE

Scripts are written in the present tense, mainly using the present simple, rather than the present continuous, for example:

Present continuous: 'John is sitting next to Martha'

Present simple: 'John sits next to Martha'

The present continuous is used to describe actions taking place over a period of time. For example, 'Matt is mending the car', i.e. he's been mending it for some time.

Look at the difference between:

```
Tom is pacing up and down the room and is running his
fingers through his hair which is long and curly.
```

and:

```
Tom paces up and down the room, running his fingers
through his long, curly hair.
```

The second version is more active, concise and visual – just what description in screenwriting should be.

THE CORRECT LAYOUT

Look at the difference between these two descriptions and layout:

1. As Tony tries frantically to open the safe door,
   Lena looks around to see if anyone is coming.

2. TONY yanks at the safe door in desperation.

   LENA bites her nails and peers out the window.

The second version gives you two shots, two mental pictures. It 'shows'; the first version 'tells'. This visual style alerts the reader to important pieces of information. (See more about layout in the next chapter.)

DIALOGUE SPLIT BY ACTION

When a character is speaking and then there's some action and then the character continues speaking, you indicate the continuation like this:

                    EMILY
        Why don't you answer me? What have I done?

Richard stares out of the window.

                  EMILY (CONT'D)
           For God's sake! Tell me!

Richard walks out of the room, without looking at her.

```
                    EMILY (CONT'D)
                     (sobbing)
      It's not my fault, Richard! He forced me!
```

CREATING SUSPENSE

If you don't engage the emotions of the audience, they won't become involved with the film. Suspense is a powerful technique to create this involvement.

Creating suspense is not difficult if you use two simple principles: anticipation and fear.

Anticipation is a simple concept: its secret lies in letting the audience think that something bad could happen. We create anticipation by introducing a situation that's fraught with the possibility of danger or risk. Here's a scenario which creates both anticipation and fear:

A teenage girl lies in bed asleep. Cut to a large garden outside. No other houses in sight. A movement in the bushes. A pair of shoes walk over the grass. Cut back to the girl who moans in her sleep. Cut back to feet creeping across the lawn to the house. An unseen fox screams. (The audience jumps.) The girl sleeps on. A window is prised open by gloved hands. The feet creep noiselessly up the stairs. A creak. The feet stop moving. The girl's eyes fly open. She listens. The feet move relentlessly on ...

This suspense is created by using an isolated location, a vulnerable girl and an unseen 'villain', and by speedy cutting from person to person. Look how the tension builds as the person moves up the stairs. We desperately want the girl to run away, but we have an awful feeling (anticipation) that she's not going to.

Hitchcock's distinction

Alfred Hitchcock made an interesting distinction between suspense and surprise. Surprise, he thought, was much inferior as a storytelling device to suspense. Something suddenly happens, there is shock, and it is over – surprise. Suspense is far more drawn-out and potent. (Look at how the writer of the film *Witness* uses suspense after an Amish boy witnesses a murder in a men's toilet. The killer looks for the boy in each cubicle. This takes some time and each time the killer throws back a cubicle door, the audience are tight with tension, terrified the man will find the boy who's standing on top of the toilet to avoid detection. That's powerful suspense.

How to present information

Suspense consists of suggesting that certain things are likely to happen and making the audience wait to see if it does. The writer allows the audience to know certain things, but not others. In fact, suspense means withholding information from the audience so that they are forced to watch the film in order to discover the outcome.

Alfred Hitchcock, of course, was a master of suspense. One of the most famous examples of suspense is the shower sequence in his 1960 film *Psycho*. While Marion Crane (Janet Leigh) takes a shower, the shadow of an old woman, with a knife in her hand, creeps towards her slowly. We know what's going to happen before the knife is plunged down repeatedly to the accompaniment of Bernard Herrmann's screeching violin score.

Resolving suspense

The important thing to remember about suspense is not to resolve it too soon so that the audience becomes tense with expectation. Build up the tension until the suspense is almost too much to bear.

> Remember: suspense creates momentum – the forward movement of your story. This vital component will keep the audience interested until the credits roll.

MANIPULATING POINT OF VIEW

A scene can be written in different ways with identical dialogue and yet create completely different reactions from the audience because of the point of view (P.O.V.) you use.

Look at the two versions below.

Version 1:

```
INT. TRUDIE'S BEDROOM – NIGHT


TRUDIE suddenly wakes. She hears voices downstairs
and creeps to the door to listen. She looks a wreck.


                    SIMON (O.C.)
            Oh God... what are we going to do?


                    TANYA (O.C.)
            I don't want to be here when she –
```

                    SIMON (O.C.)
          goes ballistic?

                    TANYA (O.C.)
          Don't you think we should say some thing?
          (BEAT)   Remember what happened last time
          she -

INT. A SITTING ROOM - NIGHT
They both gasp as Trudie pokes her head around the
door and glares at them jealously.

Version 2:

INT. A SITTING ROOM - NIGHT
Tanya and Simon are sitting close together, reading
a newspaper article. The headline reads.

THEIR P.O.V. ACTRESS BOMBS ON FIRST NIGHT.
Underneath the headline is a glossy photo of a
scantily dressed, sexy-looking actress.

                    SIMON
          Oh God... what are we going to do?

                    TANYA
          I don't want to be here when she -

                    SIMON
          goes ballistic?

                    TANYA
          Don't you think we should say some thing?
          (BEAT) Remember what happened last time
          she -

They gasp as the door opens. TRUDIE, the woman in the
photo, glares at them jealously. She now looks a
wreck.

In both versions, we hear the same dialogue but because I've
shown the scene from a different viewpoint in Version 2, we have
a completely different reaction to what is really happening. In
Version 1, we identify with Trudie because we see everything from
her point of view. We think that Simon and Tanya are conspiring
against her (or even having an affair) by the way they gasp when
she walks in. But in Version 2 we have a completely different
reaction to Trudie. She's obviously a difficult actress who's
'bombed' on the stage before and they're really worried about her
finding out.

> Remember: the details you choose to show the audience influence
> how they 'see' your story. Think about this when you're writing your
> own scenes.

CREATING FAST PACING

Look how cutting from one scene to another creates tension and
excitement in the following extract.

INT. A BLACK BMW – DAY
The CLICK of a rifle-catch of a Johnson Redi Mag 11.
AN UNSEEN MAN breathes noisily.

The unseen man SQUEEZES down on the catch lever. The
magazine SNICKS into position, ready to fire.

EXT. OUTSIDE BLACK BMW –DAY

FOUR HEAVY-SET MEN sit tensely inside the car, all carrying guns. They check their watches.

INT. BLACK BMW - DAY

                    MAN 1
                One minute.

The other three men nod to him, then put stockings over their heads.

EXT. A STREET - DAY

A 6-YEAR-OLD BOY and HIS MOTHER run down the street holding hands and laughing. The small boy holds a ball in his other hand. He suddenly breaks away from his mother and runs around a corner.

EXT. OUTSIDE THE BANK - DAY

The men LEAP out of the car athletically.

The boy's ball rolls towards them in SLOW MOTION.

Three men race towards the glass doors of the bank in slow motion. The fourth, falls over the ball and SMASHES into a wall in slow motion.

The mother and child stare at him, rigid with horror.

INT. BANK - DAY

Normal time. Glass doors EXPLODE OPEN. The three men
BURST in and fire bullets into the ceiling. The sound
is terrifying.

                    MAN 1
                HIT THE FLOOR - NOW

Everyone in the bank hits the floor.

SILENCE

The men stare at each other in alarm, realizing that
MAN 4 isn't with them.

A gun shot outside the bank. Everyone tenses.

                    MAN 2
                  Shit!

Can you see how cutting from a close-up of the gun to an exterior
view of the car (where we see the four gangsters) creates tension?
Then by cutting to the happy mother and child (who we
anticipate will become caught up in the coming violence) even
more tension is created.

Look how I've used active verbs for fast pacing: the unseen man
'squeezes'; the magazine ' snicks'; the son and his mother 'run';
glass doors 'explode'; the men 'leap' and 'race'.

Remember, all the powerful techniques mentioned in this chapter will elevate your script out of the amateur slush pile, often read by junior script readers, and into the professional one, read by producers and agents.

EXERCISES

1. Write the first 40 pages of your screenplay.
2. Make sure you have your first Turning Point.
3. Don't forget to use foreshadowing and suspense to create tension.
4. Think carefully about the length and layout of each scene and the point of view you use.

8

Writing Effective Dialogue

MAKING DIALOGUE REAL

Your characters need to sound real, but remember, real people don't speak in complete, formal sentences. Go to a public place and listen to people speaking. More importantly, notice the differences in the way people speak. Take note of the cadence of people's speech, their slang and their unstructured, informal tone.

Listen in on conversations and you'll discover that there is often one who leads and one who follows. The next time you hear two people talking, take careful note: who has the upper hand? How is it articulated?

MAKING DIALOGUE EFFECTIVE

Here's what a writer must learn to do with dialogue to make it effective.

1. Reveal nuances of a character's personality by showing what motivates him or her.

2. Find words crisply suited to each individual character's personality.

3. Use dialogue where characters are sometimes speaking at cross purposes and interrupting each other.

4. Use subtext to show what's simmering beneath the surface.

5. Use some characters who have a sense of humour.

6. Suggest relationships by how a character speaks to another,
    i.e. look at the different way a mother speaks to her children/
    her sibling or her husband.

7. Establish conflict.

8. Drip-feed small fragments of your character's backstory into
    the dialogue.

9. Use dialogue that moves the story forward.

I'm sure that this list looks daunting, so I'm going to show you
examples of how you can incorporate these points in your own
dialogue.

Remember: every scene you write with characters in it should show
what is motivating them, so think about the emotions of the
characters within each scene, then you will know exactly how they
will act and speak.

Example 1

INT. ADVERTISING OFFICE. NIGHT

SUSAN is working on a project when TIM comes in and
stares at her. She looks up.

                    SUSAN
        What's up?

                    TIM
        Why are you still here? It's

getting dark. You shouldn't
walk home by yourself.

                SUSAN
Why not?

She gets up and walks over to him, a little too close.

                TIM
You know why not.

                SUSAN
You're not wearing your ring.

                TIM
             (beat)
I should go.

She's very close now.

                SUSAN
Why?

                TIM
Mary's late.

                SUSAN
          (surprised)
She's picking you up here?

                TIM
No, she's (beat) late.

SUSAN sucks in her breath and stares at him.

```
                SUSAN
      You bastard. You told me you were
      living like a monk.


He can't look at her.
```

Can you see how much we know about them through this short exchange which is full of subtext? It's obvious Tim is worried about something when he walks into her office as he looks at her but doesn't speak. We can tell from her reaction that this is unusual. It's obvious they're having a relationship because of Susan's body language and her reaction to Tim's news. We know a lot about their personalities: Susan is afraid of nothing; Tim is a weak philanderer.

This scene is powerful because their dialogue doesn't follow a pattern of question and answer – it changes direction – just as real conversations do between people who know each other well. It's also powerful because the dialogue is full of subtext: pregnancy and marriage aren't mentioned once, but we know Tim's back story: he's married and his wife is pregnant. We also know from Tim's reaction to Susan's 'you told me you were living like a monk' that Tim feels embarrassed because he's lied to Susan about his relationship with his wife. (And, obviously to his wife about Susan.)

> Remember: once you know how your character thinks, your dialogue will flow from them, not you. The best dialogue springs from knowing your character's personality in depth.

Example 2

Two lovers are saying goodbye at the train station. We don't want the dialogue to be 'on the nose', i.e. explicit, so again, we're going to use subtext to show their grief.

```
INT. A TRAIN STATION - NIGHT
The station is packed with people. A young couple,
SIMON and CLARE, stand apart, not looking at each
other.

                   SIMON
         I thought you said the train left
         at 6.30.

                   CLARE
         I don't know what time it leaves.

                   SIMON
                 (angry)
         6.30 you said! Look at the time!

Simon glares at the station clock.

                   CLARE
                (shouting)
         I don't want to look at the time!

They stare at each other in silence and suddenly
their faces crumple with pain.
```

Instead of having a sentimental scene of hugging and kissing, we show two lovers arguing because time is running out for them.

There are many ways to use subtext. In *Brief Encounter* (1945), there's a scene in a café between two lovers (Celia Johnson and Trevor Howard) who have to say goodbye silently because a talkative friend suddenly joins them. Using a third character (who's blissfully unaware of the pain of the other characters) makes the scene both powerful and memorable. We know exactly what the lovers are feeling, although none of their emotions are expressed in dialogue.

Remember: dialogue isn't made up of words alone. Silences are as important and, sometimes, more important for conveying emotions.

Well-written subtext allows the audience to engage with characters: 'on the nose' dialogue does the opposite.

AVOIDING 'ON THE NOSE' DIALOGUE

Overstated (bad) dialogue is called 'on the nose'. Here's a scene between a father and his son who's being bullied.

```
                    SON
          Dad, the kids at school are
          bullying me again.


                    DAD
          I'll soon sort that out. I'll call
          your Headmaster.


                    SON
          But you've been in already and all
          he did was talk to them and they
          denied doing it.
```

```
                    DAD
         It will be different this time,
         I'm sure of it. Your Headmaster is
         a reasonable chap. Leave it to me.
```

Characters who know each other well don't spell everything out
for each other – they use a form of shorthand. In this scene we're
being told too much.

Here's a tighter version.

```
                    SON
          They did it again.


                    DAD
          I'm calling the Head.


                    SON
          No – you'll only make it worse.


                    DAD
          So what can I do?


                    SON
          Nothing.
```

The audience have to work a little harder, but only a little because
you'll give them plenty of visual information. The boy's clothes
will be torn, there'll be blood on his face and you'll show by the
father's body language how helpless he feels when his son says
'Nothing.'

Remember: economical dialogue laced with subtext and visual details are vital ingredients to add when writing a great screenplay.

AVOIDING FEEDER LINES

Be careful you don't allow any of your characters to 'feed' lines to another. Here's an example of what I mean:

```
INT. A NEWSPAPER OFFICE - DAY
Two reporters sit at their desks, chatting.

                    PAUL
          You'll never guess where I saw Sir
          Michael Crompton yesterday.


                    SHEILA
          Where?


                    PAUL
          In Sam Brown's office.


                    SHEILA
          I wonder what he was doing there?


                    PAUL
          Working on the new Thames project.
```

Sheila serves no purpose other than to allow Paul to give us information which makes the scene static and dull.

If you have a lot of vital information that the audience needs to understand the story, sprinkle it throughout your script so it seems organic to the action and the characters. However, if you have a

little, such as the above scene, give the information to characters
who actively react to each other. For example:

> PAUL
> You'll never guess where I saw Sir
> Michael Crompton yesterday.

> SHEILA
> Sam Brown's office. He's
> working on the new Thames project.

> PAUL
> (amazed)
> How the hell do you know that?

> SHEILA
> I'm clairvoyant.

> PAUL
> So who tipped you off?

Now the dialogue is edgier. There's a frisson of rivalry between
two reporters who both want a story and know each other well.

UNUSUAL DIALOGUE FORMATS

Dual dialogue
Dual-column dialogue (dual dialogue) is used when two people
are talking simultaneously. This is how it's written. (You need to
use script software to set up the formatting.)

AMY	ROB
(into mobile)	(into phone)
Yeah, 4 million! Rob	Mum -- are you still
fainted when he heard	there? No, it's not a
'cos it's the first time	joke. I've won 4
he's bought a ticket! Can	million pounds! Tell
you imagine!	Dad! Tell everyone!

If you have a character speaking and someone interrupts half way through, you write it like this:

                     AMY
        You know you asked me to marry you
        and I said -

AMY	ROB
(continuing)	
I wouldn't because I'm	You wouldn't because
not the person you think	you think I don't know
am.	what sort of person I
	you are.

DIALOGUE AND BODY LANGUAGE

Remember that your characters are not standing still when they're speaking. Think of their emotions in each scene and you'll know exactly what they're doing. For example, if a man makes love to a woman and then immediately gets up and walks out, leaving her alone, we know that this man doesn't want a real relationship with the woman – he just wants sex. If the woman clings onto him as he tries to leave, we know she's insecure and that the relationship is doomed.

Remember: make all your character's body language resonate with the audience. Each character's body language should give visual clues about their personalities.

EXERCISE

Print out all the pages you've written so far and erase the character's name. Do you know who is speaking? If you know your characters well, you will. If you don't, read Chapter I again and work on all the character questions in detail until you find each character's 'voice'. This is an important exercise.

Loglines

WHAT IS A LOGLINE?

A logline is a very short summary of your story (one to three sentences). It's crucially important to write an excellent logline because this is a powerful marketing tool to interest an agent or producer. The producer will then use this logline to get funding for your script. That's how important it is.

Loglines are often confused with taglines. These are the one-line straplines you read on billboards and in cinemas like 'Not every gift is a blessing' (*Sixth Sense*) or 'The movie too HOT for words' (*Some Like it Hot*).

WHAT DOES A LOGLINE DO?

In contrast, a logline should tell the reader three things: who the lead character is; what his problem is; how he is going to solve it, i.e. the who, what, how of the story. The logline should show that the lead character has a problem and must achieve a certain goal in order to solve that problem.

Here are some examples of loglines that work.

'A shy young boy discovers a stranded alien and finds the courage to defy the authorities to help it return to its home planet.' (*E.T.*)

'After a high-powered surgeon is wrongly convicted of murdering his wife, he escapes custody and hunts down the real killer – a one-armed man.' (*The Fugitive*).

'When a powerful gangster is gunned down, his reluctant son must seek revenge and take over the family business.' *The Godfather*).

In all three loglines, we know who the protagonist is, what his dilemma is and, most importantly, what his goal is. What we have above is essentially the *spine* of the story – the sentence the entire film hangs on.

A logline should not 'tell' the reader the whole story, but show that you have an exciting, well-structured plot. All three films have far more plot than we are giving in the logline, but it doesn't matter. We have to break the whole film down into a simple selling tool.

HOW LOGLINES WORK

These loglines work because they clearly shows the who, the what and the how of the story.

E.T.
- ◆ **Who**: shy young boy.
- ◆ **What**: discovers an isolated alien and wants to help him.
- ◆ **How**: he defies the authorities and does.

The Fugitive
- ◆ **Who**: a high-powered surgeon.
- ◆ **What**: wrongly convicted of murdering his wife.
- ◆ **How**: he escapes custody and hunts down the real killer.

The Godfather

◆ **Who**: a son (Michael Corleone).

◆ **What**: his father is gunned down.

◆ **How**: he seeks revenge and ends up running the family 'business'.

You must be able to reduce your story to a simple who, what and how. This can be done even in a story as complex as *The Godfather* which is full of vivid characters and subplots. On the surface, the film is about Don Corleone, but when you study it more closely, its essence is the descent of Michael Corleone, from all-American hero into a mobster who takes over the family 'business', and who becomes the main character in two more Godfather films.

WRITING AN EFFECTIVE LOGLINE

Make every word in your logline work hard by using active verbs. Look at the active verbs used in the three loglines above; 'defy', 'escapes', 'hunts', 'is gunned'. Such words show that your protagonist is active and the story is going to be exciting.

Remember: if you have a good story, you will be able to extract its essence. If you can't, you either haven't got one or you haven't structured it properly. If your idea has 'legs', go back to your step outline and restructure it.

Using the 'who', the 'what' and the 'how' formula is incredibly useful when writing loglines, but if your story is a complex sci-fi, you might need the 'set up' to make sense of it. For example:

'In a future where criminals are arrested before the crime

occurs, a despondent cop struggles to prove his innocence for a murder he has not yet committed.' (*Minority Report*.)

If you leave out the first clause, the logline wouldn't make sense.

USING THE LOGLINE AS YOUR SALES PITCH

The logline is your sales pitch, the first thing you write in a query letter or the pitch you use on the phone.

There is tremendous competition in the film world so make sure your story has a great hook, i.e. an idea that jumps off the page. Think – what sets *your* script apart from all other scripts that have a similar basis? What is unique about your characters and how they react to the events? What is its USP, i.e. Unique Selling Point? There have been thousands of stories written in every genre, so what's different about yours?

> Remember: think about what's at stake for your protagonist if he doesn't achieve his goal and make those stakes high.

There are a number of places on the Internet that will help you write great loglines. Perhaps the best is www.imdb.com. There are hundreds of loglines from every film listed on this site – some good, some not so good. Once you've logged onto the first page, go to Search and click on Titles. Then type the name of the film you're looking for. Click on Go and you'll see lists of Genre, Tagline (used on billboards to advertise the film), Plot, Awards, etc. Strangely, the logline of the film is listed under Plot! I have no idea why. You will also find a synopsis of the film, details of the cast and crew, and film reviews. This is an incredibly useful site.

TIPS WHEN WRITING A LOGLINE

1. Use the present tense.

2. Try to avoid adverbs.

3. Don't use names (unless your protagonist is famous, e.g. Captain Cook).

4. Use a well-chosen adjective to describe your protagonist like 'high-powered', 'angst-ridden', 'loner', etc.

5. Make sure you identify his adversary, i.e. his antagonist.

EXERCISE

Now practise writing loglines for your script. Use the present tense, strong verbs and avoid adverbs.

Remember: you may have to do this 40 times to get it right, but the effort will be well worth it.

Film Genres

In this chapter we look at some of the characteristics of the major film genres.

ACTION

Action and adventure films are the most financially successful genres to work within. The main characteristics include the following:

- There is a concentration on high energy physical stunts and chases.

- Most have non-stop action with simplistic plots, with the good guys battling against the bad.

- This genre is pure escapism, e.g. *Kill Bill, Volumes 1 & 2*.

ADVENTURE

Adventure films are usually exciting stories with new experiences or exotic locales, very similar to or often paired with the action film genre. They can include traditional swashbucklers, serialized films and historical spectacles (similar to the epic film genre), searches or expeditions for lost continents, 'jungle' and 'desert' epics, treasure hunts, disaster films or searches for the unknown.

The main characteristics include the following:

- The protagonist must frequently save the world (or part of it).

- He is attractive, physically and mentally, i.e. he appeals to the audience.

- This genre is fast-paced and plot-intensive, containing a huge number of physical and mental challenges for the hero.

- His antagonist is a supreme villain with formidable powers.

ANIMATION

Walt Disney made this genre popular in the 1930s and it has now become popular again with films like *The Lion King*, *Shrek*, *Finding Nemo*, *Bee Movie* (which has the unique story of a bee who sues humans for eating honey!) and *Ratatouille* (which has the unique idea of a rat being a chef!). Many films now combine 'reality' with animation like *Enchanted* and *The Golden Compass*. This popularity has been helped enormously by CGI (computer-generated imagery).

COMEDY

There are a wide variety of sub-genres in comedy, but the one thing they all have in common is a plot which is designed to amuse and provoke laughter by exaggerating the situation, the language, action, relationships and characters. Comedy can be:

- slapstick like *The Deserter* (2003);

- sophisticated like *Annie Hall* (1977);

- teen like *It's A Boy Girl Thing* (2006);

- dark and complex like *American Beauty* (1990);

- romantic like *Four Weddings and a Funeral* (1994);

- surreal like *Monty Python and the Holy Grail* (1975).

CRIME/GANGSTER

Crime (gangster) films are developed around the sinister actions of criminals or mobsters, particularly bank-robbers, underworld figures or ruthless hoodlums who operate outside the law, stealing and murdering their way through life. Criminal and gangster films are often categorized as film noir or detective-mystery films because of underlying similarities between these cinematic forms. Films like the *Godfather* films, *The Long Good Friday*, *Goodfellas*, *Scarface*, *Pulp Fiction*, *The Departed* and *The Sinatra Club* fall into this category.

This category includes a description of various 'serial killer' films.

DRAMA

The main characteristics are:

♦ serious plot and character combined stories;

♦ three-dimensional characters, settings and situations;

♦ intense character development and interaction.

Dramatic films are probably the largest film genre, with many subsets: *Mrs Doubtfire* is listed as a family drama; *L.A. Confidential* as a police drama; *ER* as a medical drama; *Boston Legal* as a legal drama; *Sense and Sensibility* as a period drama; *The Green Mile* as a prison drama; *West Wing* as a political drama; and *The Road to Guantanamo* as a docu-drama.

EPIC

Epics include costume dramas, historical dramas, war films, medieval romps or 'period pictures' that often cover a large expanse of time set against a vast, panoramic backdrop. The main characteristics are as follows:

◆ Sharing elements of the elaborate adventure films genre.

◆ Using a historical or imagined event, and a mythic, legendary or heroic figure.

◆ Adding an extravagant setting and lavish costumes.

◆ Using spectacle, high production values and a sweeping musical score.

FANTASY

Fantasy films often take us on a fairy-like journey into strange mythological worlds where incredible things happen. They have elements of magic, myth and folklore which often appeal to both children and adults. This genre has become very popular with films like the *Superman* films, *Time Bandits*, *Spider-Man*, *X Men*, *Venedetta*, *The Lord of the Rings*, *Beowolf*, *Enchanted* and *The Golden Compass*, and the franchise films of *Harry Potter*.

Interestingly, three of the top five box-office performers in Moviemeter's November 2007 list were films in this category: *Enchanted*, *Beowolf* and *The Golden Compass*.

FILM NOIR

Film noir comprises a dark, brooding vision of urban existence, often built around the nature of betrayal. Its main characteristics are as follows:

◆ The central character inhabits a world of danger or risk, i.e. they are usually on the fringes of society.

◆ The protagonist believes that their chance of happiness lies in a sexual relationship with another person.

◆ This other person usually betrays them (becomes their antagonist).

◆ However, the real 'villain' is the city in which they live; it destroys the possibility of honest relationships.

HORROR

Horror films are designed to frighten and to invoke our hidden worst fears, often in a terrifying, shocking finale, while captivating and entertaining us at the same time in a cathartic experience. Its main characteristics are as follows:

◆ The central character is usually a victim.

◆ Violence and sexuality are rampant in this genre.

◆ The location is paramount, e.g. the house built on a cemetery.

◆ Part or all of the final 'resolution' will spring from the supernatural or irrational.

However, the horror film genre has a wide range of styles, from the earliest silent *Nosferatu* classic, to today's CGI monsters and deranged humans. They are often combined with science fiction when the menace or monster is related to a corruption of technology, or when Earth is threatened by aliens. There are many sub-genres of horror: slasher, teen terror, serial killers, satanic, Dracula, Frankenstein, etc.

Mist, adapted from a short story by Stephen King, grossed $12.9 million in one month in 2007. *The Mummy: Tomb of the Dragon Emperor*, release date 6 August 2008 topped that figure considerably. It grossed $399,855 in its opening weekend in the USA. However, both films were over-shadowed by *The Dark Knight* which grossed $529,696 in 2008.

MUSICAL

Musical/dance films are cinematic forms that emphasize full-scale scores or song and dance routines in a significant way (usually with a musical or dance performance integrated as part of the film narrative), or they are films that are centred on combinations of music.

SCIENCE FICTION

Sci-fi films are often quasi-scientific, visionary and imaginative – complete with heroes, aliens, distant planets, impossible quests, improbable settings, fantastic places, great dark and shadowy villains, futuristic technology, unknown and unknowable forces and extraordinary monsters ('things or creatures from space'), either created by mad scientists or by nuclear havoc.

The main characteristics are as follows:

- The protagonist is generally an innocent victim.

- He or she may not defeat the antagonist by the end of the film.

- The antagonist may not be human.

- The humans are usually ennobled by their attempt to survive.

- This genre is generally plot-driven rather than character-oriented.

Science fiction often expresses the potential of technology to destroy humankind and easily overlaps with horror films, particularly when technology or alien life forms become malevolent as in *The Terminator*.

> Sci-fi films are sometimes an offshoot of fantasy films, or they share some similarities with action/adventure films.

THRILLER

The main characteristics of this genre include:

- a high level of anticipation;

- nerve wracking tension and suspense;

- fast pacing;

- resourceful protagonists;

- complicated twists and turns in the storyline.

Here are a few of its sub-genres with examples:

- psychological thrillers – *Psycho* (1960), *Sixth Sense* (1999);

- political thrillers – *The Quiet American* (2002), *V for Vendetta* (2005);

- psycho-thrillers – *Silence of the Lambs* (1991), *Collateral* (2004);

- erotic thriller – *Blue Velvet* (1986), *Basic Instinct* (1992);

- police thrillers – *The French Connection* (1971), *Dirty Harry* (1971).

WAR

War films acknowledge the horror and heartbreak of war, letting the actual combat fighting (against nations or humankind) on land, sea or in the air provide the primary plot or background for the action of the film. War films are often paired with other genres, such as action, adventure, drama, romance, comedy (black) and even Westerns. They often take a denunciatory approach toward warfare. They may include POW tales, stories of military operations and training.

WESTERN

This is one of the oldest genres and has undergone a resurgence in popularity with films like *Dances with Wolves*, *Unforgiven* and *Brokeback Mountain*.

MINOR SUB-GENRES

These include:

- aviation films;
- buddy films;
- caper films;
- 'chick flicks';
- detective/mystery;
- espionage films;
- jungle films;
- legal films;
- martial arts films;
- medical films;
- military films;
- parody films;
- police films;
- political films;
- prison films;
- religious films;
- slasher films;
- swashbucklers etc.

COMBINING GENRES

Your script can combine two genres, e.g. Romantic Comedy or Historical Thriller, but if you need three or more genres to describe your story, you need to go back to your outline and rework it. (Although once it's in production, the film can be listed under four or five genres – see imdb.com.)

In contrast, the auteur system creates films which are the 'vision' of one person, usually the director, because his or her indelible style, authorial vision or 'signature' dictates the personality, look and feel of the film. Certain directors (and actors) are known for certain types of films. For example, Woody Allen is linked with comedy, Alfred Hitchcock with suspense and thrillers, M. Night Shyamalan with the supernatural and John Ford with westerns.

Professional Script Formatting

If you don't submit your screenplay in the correct format it will, most probably, end up in someone's waste bin. However, it's now easier than ever to make your screenplay look professional by buying screenwriting software (see Appendix 2).

BASIC PRINCIPLES

The following are the basic principles for professional script formatting.

1. Use the correct typeface. Screenplays are always written in 12-pt Courier. This font is standard in the industry and no other font will do.

2. One page of a script typed on A4 in 12-pt Courier, properly formatted, will roughly equal a minute of screen time. In order to appear professional, it is important that your script be of a proper length. Feature film scripts have some flexibility, but they should generally be within the 100–120 page range. (Ignore the fact that epics like *Braveheart* and *Titanic* were much longer – far too long many would argue.) However, comedy scripts tend to be shorter – around 90 pages.

3. Don't use camera directions unless you are also going to direct your own screenplay. Camera directions are one of the director's jobs. However, you can learn how to 'direct' the director in a subtle way as I've shown you in Chapter 7.

4. Don't number your scenes. Scripts are only given scene numbers when they are budgeted and scheduled to be shot.

5. The title page should contain the title of the script, your name, address, e-mail address, telephone number and agent (if you have one). The title should be typed in capital letters. I use 14-point Courier for the title, but know people who only use 12-point. Don't type your name in capital letters – it looks pretentious. You can register your script if you want to. I always register my scripts with WGA (the Writer's Guild of America). You can do this online.

6. You don't need to include a cast list (as you do for TV and stage plays). Just the title page and the script.

7. Use plain white covers, front and back. Don't be tempted to write in a fancy font to impress people – it won't. They'll think you're an amateur who doesn't know much about screenwriting.

8. Bind your script simply. American screenplays are printed single-sided on three-hole-punched letter-sized (8.5 × 11 inch) paper, and held together with two brass brads in the top and bottom hole. The middle hole is left empty. In the UK, scripts are printed single-sided, but double-hole-punched using A4 paper (although some UK writers use the US letter paper format when their scripts are to be read by American producers). I use two-piece filing clips. I also put sticky white tape on the back of the clips for two reasons: it stops the clips opening and prevents producers being annoyed. A producer once told me that clips and brads on the back of scripts caught in everything on his desk and drove him mad.

9. All screenplays begin with FADE IN:

10. SCENE HEADINGS, or slug lines, indicate whether the location is an interior (INT) or exterior (EXT), the location, and whether it is day or night. Occasionally, a scene is both interior and exterior, as in a doorway or at a window, and this is expressed as:

INT/EXT. A LIFT - NIGHT

If the location encompasses a large area, such as Arsenal Football Ground, then the writer needs to specify a certain area, such as ON THE BENCH or AT FIFTY YARD LINE.

11. You always need to tell the reader what time of time it is: day or night. The day or night designation is for shoot scheduling purposes and needs to be straightforward. Subtler distinctions in time should be indicated in the text of the scene description. Occasionally, additional information needs to be included in the scene heading such as the season or year. Put this in parenthesis after the location.

EXT. LONDON BRIDGE (1942) - DAY

12. CUT TO: Some writers never use CUT TO: arguing that the transition is implied by moving from one scene to another. Other writers use CUT TO: after almost every scene which isn't a good idea as this will lengthen your script considerably. Reserve the use of CUT TO: for abrupt changes in location, or for cutting back and forth from different locations during an action sequence. It makes the action look more exciting.

13. DISSOLVE TO: Use this sparingly if you want one scene to be gradually replaced, i.e. 'dissolved' into another.

14. FADE OUT. Used to end all scripts.

15. SCENE DESCRIPTION is always double-spaced down from the scene heading. (This will be formatted for you by your software.) The scene description or action should be brief, powerful and, above all, visual (as already discussed in Chapter 6).

16. PARAGRAPH LAYOUT. Here you have greatest flexibility. Use it creatively as the layout has a great impact on the way your description reads. Don't write dense blocks of prose as something important might be skimmed over. (Look at the variety of layouts from films in Chapter 5.) Develop your own strong individual style which is clear, concise and visual.

17. CAPITALIZATION. When characters are first introduced their names need to be capitalized. Thereafter, in the descriptive passages, their names appear in upper and lower case. This serves as a device to assist casting directors, script supervisors and performers.

18. SOUND CUES. When sound cues are used the first word in the cue needs to be capitalized to alert the sound technician skimming the script that his expertise is going to be needed here, e.g. 'The phone RINGS', 'The cars CRASH'.

19. VOICE OVER (V.O.) is used when dialogue is put over a scene either through narration, a character thinking out loud or when a tape recording is played in a scene.

20. OFF SCREEN (O.S.) is used when a character is heard but not seen, as when a character talks from another room in a house or is simply out of the camera frame.

    Both (V.O.) and (O.S.) appear abbreviated, capitalized and in parentheses directly after the character cue.

21. SMALL ROLES. Actors with small roles are sometimes given numbers such as GIRL 1 and GIRL 2.

22. PARENTHETICALS. have already been discussed this in Chapter 7. Use sparingly.

23. BEAT. This is used to denote a small pause or hesitation in a speaker.

24. DIALOGUE format. Some basic rules for dialogue writing to remember:
    (a) Spell out two digit numbers, personal titles, and indications of time.
    (b) Don't hyphenate long words.
    (c) Don't break a sentence from one page to the next. When a long passage of dialogue needs to be continued onto another page type (MORE) at the character cue tab and then (CONT'D) after the character cue on the following page. If you use Final Draft you won't ever have to worry about this problem as the software sorts it out for you automatically. (However, the use of MORE seems to be slowly disappearing.)

25. MONTAGE. The montage is formatted as a single shot, but involves different locations. It isn't necessary to write END OF MONTAGE – it will be obvious.
    (a) Jamie is born in a hospital room. The midwife cleans him

and hands him over to his smiling mother.

(b) Jamie rolls over on the carpet. His mother claps.

(c) Holding on to the coffee table, Jamie takes his first steps. His overjoyed mother hugs him.

(d) Jamie runs manically around the room. His exhausted mother slumps on a settee, watching him.

26. A SERIES OF SHOTS is similar to a montage, but it usually takes place in one location and relates to the same action, e.g. the beginning of a hurricane:

(a) Shop windows start to rattle and shake.

(b) Hanging signs swing back and forth.

(c) Bricks and shards of glass begin to fall onto the pavement.

(d) People run for cover.

27. SHORT LINES/POETRY/LYRICS. If a character is reciting some poetry, or singing a song, you need to write the dialogue in short lines as follows:

>   DAISY
>   Mary, Mary, quite contrary,
>   How does your garden grow,
>   With silver bells and cockle shells
>   And pretty maids all in a row.

Song lyrics are typically written in all caps.

>   DAISY
>   (singing)
>   ROW, ROW, ROW YOUR BOAT
>   GENTLY DOWN THE STREAM
>   MERRILY, MERRILY, MERRILY, MERRILY
>   LIFE IS BUT A DREAM.

28. TELEPHONE CONVERSATIONS. Writers are often confused as to how telephone conversations should be written. Here's a simple way to categorize them:

(a) one-sided in one location;

(b) two-sided in one location;

(c) two-sided in two locations.

Below is the same example using three different layouts.

(a) One-sided in one location:

```
INT. CHRISTINE'S OFFICE - NIGHT


CHRIS types fast on a computer. The phone RINGS. She
carries on typing. The phone keeps RINGING.
Sighing, she picks it up.

                    CHRIS
          Yes? ... You've been what? I don't
          believe this! This is the second time
          this week you've done this to
          me... you promised to pick them up
          this morning... oh, my work
          doesn't matter - is that
          what you're saying?
```

(b) A two-sided in one location: This time we hear what Jeremy is saying, but can't see him:

```
INT. CHRIS'S OFFICE - NIGHT


CHRIS types fast on a computer. The phone RINGS. She
carries on typing. The phone keeps RINGING.
Sighing, she picks it up.
```

           CHRIS
Yes?

         JEREMY (O.S.)
Sorry darling. I've been held up.

           CHRIS
You've been what!

         JEREMY (O.S.)
If you'll just listen for a minute.

           CHRIS
I don't believe this!

         JEREMY (O.S.)
I can't help it.

           CHRIS
This is the 2nd time this week
you've done this to me! You
promised to pick them up this
morning!

         JEREMY (O.S.)
I know, I'm really sorry, darling
but I can't. You'll have to. The
boss has just given me this deadline.

           CHRIS
Oh, my work doesn't matter. Is
that what you're saying?

Does hearing Jeremy alter anything in this scene? If hearing the other character doesn't give dramatic tension or tell the audience something important, don't use this formatting.

(c) Two-sided in two locations: This formatting usually presents the most confusion for writers – do you need to write each 'cut' into your screenplay? The answer is no, unless there is dramatic tension if you cut back to the second location. (But don't overdo the cutting backwards and forwards as new scene headings will only slow down the read.)

However, if it's important to your story for the audience to see both locations, use this formatting:

INT. CHRIS'S OFFICE – NIGHT

CHRIS types fast on a computer. The phone RINGS. She carries on typing. The phone keeps RINGING. Sighing, she picks it up.

                    CHRIS
          Yes?

                    JEREMY (O.S.)

          Sorry darling. I've been held up –

                    CHRIS
          You've been what!

INT. JEREMY'S OFFICE - NIGHT

                    JEREMY
        If you'll just listen a minute.
SAMANTHA, Jeremy's secretary leans over his desk to
kiss him. He responds, then pushes her away,
playfully. She walks behind his desk.

                    CHRIS (O.S.)
            This is the second time this week
            you've done this to me! You
            promised to pick them up this
            morning!

Samantha leans down and blows in Jeremy's ear. He
suppresses a laugh.

                    JEREMY
            I know, I'm really sorry, darling,
            but I can't. You'll have to. The
            boss has just given me this
            deadline.

                    CHRIS (O.S.)
            Oh, my work doesn't matter. Is
            that what you're saying?

Now, the scene has a great deal of tension. Seeing what
Jeremy is doing in his office shows the relationship
between Chris and Jeremy in a completely new light,
although the dialogue is exactly the same. Think carefully
what you want to show the audience and what you want
to leave out. If you don't want the audience to know

Jeremy is having an affair, then, of course, it's better to use the earlier scene. However, audiences often like having more knowledge than one of the characters so showing Jeremy's secretary will create empathy for Chris.

29. INTERCUTS are used in phone calls when switching back and forth between two or more scenes quickly and repetitively (often used in action films to create excitement).

If it's not important who we see on the screen, use 'Intercut' and let the director or editor decide how to do it. Like this:

EXT. A BUSY STREET – DAY

DEBBIE, an undercover policewoman, hits a number on her mobile and listens. She's watching a man on the other side of the street.

Intercut with...

INT. D.C. WILLARD'S OFFICE – DAY

D.C. WILLARD grabs the phone at the first ring.

                    D.C. WILLARD
        Can you see him?

                    DEBBIE
        Yes.

Often the Intercut will end at the next Scene Heading. If you want the intercutting to end in one of the locations you've been using, just reuse that Scene Heading. For example:

> D.C. WILLARD
>
> Don't lose him.

> DEBBIE
>
> I won't, but get back-up here fast.

Debbie strides across the road as the man turns a corner.

> D.C. WILLARD
> (to his assistant)
> Get Boyce and Massey down there fast!

EXT. CORNER OF BUSY STREET – DAY

Debbie turns the corner. The man is nowhere to be seen. She swears.

Remember: the correct professional formatting will always mark you as a professional, so make sure your script looks perfectly presented. However, bear in mind that your script is only the beginning of a collaborative process – it will go through many different stages with the input of producers, directors, and technicians who mark the script with scene numbers and camera angles as an organisational tool, (although only, of course, after your script has been optioned and is going into production).

Organizations that Help Screenwriters

THE AMERICAN SCRIPTWRITING ASSOCIATION
Website: www.asascreenwriters.com

The organization is committed to supporting writers from around the world. It also sponsors the ASA/WD International Screenwriting Competition and the Annual Selling to Hollywood conference. Fees depend of the level of membership you require. See the website for more information.

THE BRITISH FILM INSTITUTE
Website: www.bfi.org.uk

The BFI has a world-renowned archive which is the largest collection of moving image material in the world. The collection includes over 275,000 films, 210,000 TV programmes, seven million photographs and 15,000 posters. (Archived material is accessible via curated exhibitions and screenings in cinemas.)

It also screens over 1,000 films a year, publishes a wide range of books on film and television, runs the BFI London Film Festival, publishes a monthly film magazine called *Sight and Sound*, and has a library which offers access to the world's largest collection of information about film and television. You can become a member of BFI and enjoy priority booking and a range of benefits for £20 a year (one of which is downloading free films).

EUROSCRIPT

Website: www.euroscript.co.uk

Euroscript was created in 1995 by the Screenwriters' Workshop, with funding from the European Union's Media II programme, with the aim of improving the quality of scripts going into production in Europe. It runs courses in scriptwriting in the UK and abroad and has a consultancy service through which writers (with money!) can pay for individual feedback on their writing. It also runs a yearly competition which costs £35. The winner of the first prize receives individual help from the treatment stage to completed screenplay via regular meetings with a script consultant plus e-mail and telephone support. Second prize is an in-depth script report, plus e-mail and telephone support. The three winners of the third prize get a bullet-point script report on any of their scripts. They also have links to organizations that offer bursaries to writers. For consultancy fees see their website.

THE FIRST FILM FOUNDATION

9 Bourlet Close, London W1W 7BP. Tel: 020 7580 2111.
E-mail: info@firstfilm.co.uk. Website: www.firstfilm.co.uk

The First Film Foundation is a charity which exists to help new writers, producers and directors to make their first feature film. It aims to provide new filmmakers with high quality development support, a link to the established film industry, and impartial, practical advice and information on how to develop a career in the film industry. Jonathan Rawlinson, the director of First Film, suggests that writers research which organizations are out there and find out exactly what they do. Organizations are more likely to help you if you've done your homework and show commitment.

INKTIP

Website: www.inktip.com

This American site was created in 2000 by Jerrol LeBaron.
Writers pay to post details of their scripts on the site. LeBaron
states:

> Over 150 production companies use the Internet to find
> scripts, with more than twenty-five per cent of these
> companies boasting good to excellent film credits. Since that
> time, the figure has greatly increased and InkTip.com has
> more than 2600 registered industry members who now have
> access to writers' scripts.

Have a look at the site and decide if you want to pay to have your
synopsis and logline on this site. Producers will request the script
if they're interested in it, (which is why it's vital to write great
synopses and loglines). As a general rule, American producers
want high-concept films which will make them money.

MEDIA UK

Website: www.mediauk.com

This site is the critically-acclaimed independent Media Directory
for the UK listing websites, addresses, telephone numbers, live
links and more, for all areas of online media. A useful site for
learning what's happening in radio, television, newspaper and the
magazine world.

THE NEW PRODUCER'S ALLIANCE

Website: www.npa.org.uk

The NPA is an international training and support provider for filmmakers. Established in 1993, the NPA is the UK national membership organization for film producers, screenwriters and directors, and a registered charity.

The NPA provides a forum and focus for over 1,000 members, ranging from film students and first-timers to highly experienced feature filmmakers, major production companies and industry affiliates.

They run regular events for screenwriters and emerging producers. Check out their website for more details.

RAINDANCE

81 Berwick Street, London W1F 8TW. Tel: 020 7287 3833

Raindance was created by Elliot Grove and is now run by a team of people who are passionately enthusiastic about independent filmmaking. They run numerous courses on writing, directing, producing and editing. In addition, they run a film festival and a number of pitching sessions (see Chapter 14).

THE ROCLIFFE FORUM

The Rocliffe New Writing Forum is a monthly platform for new writing in the UK and also runs a networking event. Rocliffe select three 7–8-minute script extracts – feature film, short film, television drama, sitcom, theatre, radio or sketches. A narrator sets the piece in context and the extracts are then performed to an industry audience of producers, development executives, directors, actors and literary agents. What Rocliffe requires from a writer is as follows:

- a 10-minute script extract (14 pages maximum) in final draft or word;

- an A4 (one-page maximum) synopsis;

- a 50-word synopsis;

- a cast breakdown and outline of each character which appears in the extract;

- an introduction to provide context, outlining where the extract fits into the overall story and clearly stating whether the script is a feature, short, television drama, sitcom or theatre;

- a short writing/industry relevant biography – 150 words maximum.

If Rocliffe accepts your extract you will hear your work being read by professional actors and get professional advice from experienced co-chairs and feedback from an audience. This could be an invaluable experience for you, but be prepared to hear criticism and answer questions.

Contact Rocliffe either by post: Rocliffe, PO Box 37344, London N1 8YB, or e-mail: scripts@rocliffe.com. If you want to reserve a place to go on the evening, e-mail: booking@rocliffe.com.
The forums now take place at BAFTA, 195 Piccadilly, London W1J 9LN. Contact them for new dates.

SCREEN DAILY
Website: www.screendaily.com

An international film news magazine that is worth subscribing to if you want up-to-date information on what film companies are producing, what they're looking for, information on sales and markets, box-office figures and distribution. It gives subscribers an in-depth knowledge of the film industry.

THE SCRIPT FACTORY

Welbeck House, 66/67 Wells Street, London W1T 3PY.
Website: www.scriptfactory.co.uk

Since 1996, The Script Factory has become one of Europe's leading development organisations working to support screenwriters by finding and developing new screenwriting talent; by supporting the people who work with screenwriters; and by presenting live screenwriting events with some of cinema's top creative talent.

Here are some of the activities they run:

*   training for screenwriters and script editors, both in the UK and abroad;

*   master classes with professional screenwriters, actors, etc.;

*   performed readings to showcase new writing;

*   script feedback;

*   a script registration service.

It is also well worth checking their website for more information.

THE SCRIPTWRITER'S NETWORK

Website: www.scriptwritersnetwork.org

This network is a voluntary non-profit organization, based in Los

Angeles. It informs members about industry news, gives opportunities for alliances with industry professionals and tries to help writers get to the next level of their career.

SHOOTING PEOPLE
Website: www.shootingpeople.org

Shooting People is an online community of filmmakers, sharing resources, skills and experience. Members post to and receive daily e-mail bulletins covering all aspects of filmmaking, add their events and screenings to the film calendars, and network with other members at parties, salons and screenings in London, New York and beyond. Members can also fill in online searchable profile cards.

Shooting People also run a screenwriting pitching network. Here you can post your logline and your synopsis of your completed script in the hope of finding an interested production company. Members pay £30 in the UK and $40 in the US. For more information, log onto the website.

SKILLSET
Website: www.skillset.org

Skillset helps the UK film industry by implementing and funding a variety of initiatives targeting new entrants and the existing workforce across the industry. They fund existing schemes that are already delivering what the industry needs, run bursaries to make it easier for freelancers to get the training they want, and create schemes to fill the gaps in current training provision. They also accredit individual courses and license successful, industry-focused training institutions to deliver training to and on behalf of the

UK film industry, including their new network of Screen Academies. Their very useful website is well worth studying.

THE SPEC SCRIPT LIBRARY
Website: www.thesource.com.au/scripts

The purpose of this Australian site is similar to that of Inktip – it connects screenwriters with producers. However, this site is free.

The Library is the largest of its type in the world. Titles/logs/ synopses of spec scripts are catalogued by the owners of the site. Then, interested parties contact the author/agent for further particulars about each script. Scripts are indexed under a huge variety of genres.

I don't know if any writers have found producers via this site, but it's worth checking its details if only because it contains a large number of synopses of varying quality.

THE STUDIO SYSTEM
Website; www.thestudiosystem.com

The Studio System is an American site which boasts it is the entertainment industry's most powerful film and television database. Subscribers enjoy unlimited access to detailed information on the people, projects and companies engaged in the development, production, release and performance of film and television content. Robust search, sort and report generation tools allow for the easy manipulation of data to fit each subscriber's needs. The Studio System's Customer Service team frequently interacts with subscribers to service research requests and offer usage tutorials. With thousands of updates published daily, The

Studio System's website states that it represents the gold standard of professional-grade film and television information.

It has also created a site called InBaseline where cast, crew and filmmakers may submit their credits for inclusion in the Baseline database. Through www.inbaseline.com, you can now ensure that your involvement in a project will be permanently acknowledged, archived and distributed to professional and consumer audiences the world over.

TAPS
Website: www.tapsnet.org

Taps is a UK organization which helps writers break into television and has strong links to all the major broadcasters and constant support from Skillset. TAPS offers professionally taught courses at accessible rates.

TAPS says it is dedicated to finding new writers and runs workshops across the UK. This has allowed them to forge tight bonds with regional broadcasters while reaching as many writers as possible. Check out their website for more details.

THE UK FILM COUNCIL
Website: www.ukfilmcouncil.org.uk

The UK Film Council is a government-backed strategic agency for film in the UK. One of the UK Film Council's main aims is to try to form long-term relationships with producers, directors and writing talent. The UK Film Council's production funds work closely together to encourage this ambition and to ensure at an early stage there is cross-fertilization of both ideas and projects.

You can approach the Film Council for money in a number of ways via their funding strands:

- Development Fund;
- New Cinema Fund;
- Premiere Fund.

Development Fund

First Feature Film Development Programme – aims to identify and support emerging filmmakers, screenwriters, writer/directors and writer/director/producer teams who have not made a feature film or who have not yet had a feature film released theatrically or broadcast on UK television. Generally, awards of up to £25,000 will be offered to screenwriters/writer-directors to write and develop a feature film.

New Cinema Fund

The New Cinema Fund encourages unique ideas, innovative approaches and new voices. The fund is aimed at financing films with passion and verve that connect with a broad range of audiences. If you have a script that's cutting edge and low budget, this is the fund to apply for.

The UK Film Council and Film Four are investing £3 million each over three years to launch the Low Budget Film Scheme in a unique initiative to generate and sustain a low-budget film industry in the UK for the first time. (The Film Company Warp X is involved with this scheme.)

Premiere Fund

The Premiere Fund is looking for projects that can capture UK and world-wide audiences. Since the inception of the UK Film

Council the Premiere Fund has invested in a wide range of successful projects that have been seen by cinema audiences around the world. *Gosford Park* directed by Robert Altman won both an Academy Award and a BAFTA award. *The Constant Gardener* directed by Fernando Meirelles won both an Academy Award and a Golden Globe for Rachel Weisz.

You will find many other films they've helped to fund on the Film Council's website.

◆ Unfortunately, the Film Council hasnow been abolished.

WOMEN IN FILM AND TV (UK)
Website: www.wftv.org.uk

WFTV works to protect and enhance the interests, status and diversity of women working at all levels in the industry and celebrate their achievement. It is a not-for-profit membership organization.

They have over 800 members covering a broad spectrum of skills and job descriptions, including, among others, lawyers, writers, accountants, directors, producers, DPs, composers, actors, make-up artists and casting directors.

If you are a woman with at least one year's professional experience in television, film or digital media, you are eligible to become a member of WFTV. See their website for more details.

WOMEN IN FILM
Website: www.wif.org

Another organization based in Los Angeles that helps women achieve in the media and entertainment industries.

THE WRITERS' GUILD OF AMERICA (WEST)
Website: www.wgaregistry.org

This is the Guild for Hollywood writers and has a membership of 9,500 film and television writers. It is famous for its registry service and registers 55,000 pieces of literary material each year. You can register a UK script online or by post to 7000 West Third St, Los Angeles, CA 90048. Online registration fees are $20 (US dollars) for non-WGAW members and $10 for members.

THE WRITERS' GUILD OF GREAT BRITAIN
15 Britannia Street, London WC1X 9JN. Tel: 020 77833 0777. Website: www.writersguild.co.uk

The Writers' Guild of Great Britain is the trade union representing writers in TV, radio, theatre, books, poetry, film and video games. There are three types of membership.

* *Student membership.* This entitles you to support and advice, the free quarterly *UK Writer* magazine, access to frequent Guild events and a weekly e-bulletin. (This membership is offered to students on an accredited writing course or on attachment to a theatre. £20 a year.)

* *Candidate membership.* This entitles you to free legal advice and vetting of contracts by Writers' Guild lawyers, support and advice, discounts on many theatre and cinema tickets, the free quarterly *UK Writer* magazine, access to frequent Guild events and a weekly e-bulletin. (This membership is offered to writers

who have not yet had at least one professional contract for writing. £100 a year.)

◆ *Full membership.* This entitles you to free legal advice and vetting of contracts by Writers' Guild lawyers, support and advice, the right to join the Guild's pension scheme and receive pension contributions from employers including the BBC and ITV, free Cannes accreditation, discounts on many theatre and cinema tickets, the free quarterly *UK Writer* magazine, access to frequent Guild events and a weekly e-bulletin. (Full membership is for writers who have at least one professional contract for writing in terms at or above the Writers' Guild minimum rates. £150 a year.)

In UK TV, film, radio and theatre, the Guild is the recognized body for negotiating minimum terms and practice agreements. It is vitally important that writers have a trade union so it is important that UK writers join this great organization.

Copywriting Your Work

COPYRIGHT AND REGISTRATION

What's the difference between copyright and registration? Here's what solicitor Stephen Aucutt* says:

> copyright is a right bestowed by law (it is the right to copy/ prevent copying); registration is a process undertaken to assist in protecting that copyright. You have an automatic copyright once you've written any piece of literary work.

So, don't become paranoid. Examples of major rip-offs are infrequent and coincidence is more likely to be responsible for the fact that another script bears a resemblance to your own rather than industrial espionage. Stephen Aucutt again:

> What needs to be remembered is that there is no copyright in an idea so the existence of two screenplays with remarkably similar plots or settings or characters does not in itself equal plagiarism. The copyright in a 'literary work' is in the actual written words, not the ideas/concept behind those words. So a screenplay set in the same place, with the same plot and similar characters of another screenplay but with entirely different dialogue may not have been copied from the other screenplay.

---

* Stephen Aucutt is a solicitor who used to work for The Writers' Guild of Great Britain.

PROTECTING YOUR SCRIPT

However, many writers want to know that their script is legally protected. There are a number of ways to do this.

◆ You could send the script to a solicitor who will lock it up in their safe for a small fee.

◆ You could register your script with an acknowledged body.

> **N.B.** *Don't seal your script and post it to yourself. This is not a fool-proof method. Professionals will argue that packages can be steamed open.*

Below are listed a number of respected organizations that offer a script registration service.

Protect Rite
Website: www.protectrite.com

This is an online registration service which will protect your script for ten years for $18.95 (US dollars). They also have a permanent registration service which costs $39.95 (US dollars). For more information log onto the website.

The Script Factory
Website: www.scriptfactory.co.uk

The Script Factory has its own tried and trusted script registration scheme where you can register your project. Three years for £30 (e-mail: stew@scriptfactory.co.uk for full details) or download a form under the heading script registration at the website.

The Script Vault
Website: www.scriptvault.com

The Script Vault offers a script registration and deposit service that helps to safeguard your copyright by registering the author of a piece of work and establishing the date it was written. This registration can prove to be invaluable in the event of a copyright dispute. It is approved by the Writers' Guild of Great Britain and only costs £10 to register a script for ten years.

The site also has some useful links to interesting articles (like 'Cannes – A Virgin's Festival Guide') and a free translation service).

The Writers' Guild of America (East)
Website: www.wgaeast.org

You can register online for $10 (US dollars) if you're a member of WGAE and $22 if you're not.

The Writers' Guild of America (West)
Website: www.wgawregistry.org

This is what the WGAW states:

> The registration process places preventative measures against plagiarism or unauthorized use of an author's material. While someone else may have the same storyline or idea in his or her material, your evidence lies in your presentation of your work. Registering your work does not disallow others from having a similar storyline or theme. Rather, registering your work would potentially discourage others from using your work without your permission.

You can register online for $20 (US dollars) if you're not a member of WGAW and for $10 if you are. British writers will be billed in UK sterling. The registration lasts for five years. For more information, log onto the website.

Marketing Your Script

LEARNING HOW TO MARKET YOUR SCRIPT

If your name isn't Sofia Coppola and your father isn't Francis Ford Coppola, you need to learn how to market your script. Remember there are thousands of other people doing what you are doing – you have to learn market strategies. Yes, I know – you're a writer, you don't want to be a business person, but the film industry is a business. It's taken me a long time to learn this fact. I naively thought it was all about creativity and talent. How you market your script (and yourself) is just as important as writing a good script.

Another thing you've got to learn is patience. Before you send your script out into the marketplace, put it in a drawer for at least a month and then re-read it. Does it read as well as it did a month ago or does it need another draft? Too often writers send out material which should be revised first. However, if you do send it out, be prepared for rejection. You'll be stunned if it's returned, but remember, the rejection is not personal. (I know it will feel like it, but it's not – they don't know you, do they?) One way to overcome rejection is through constant writing. By the time you receive an answer from a production company you should be deep into your next script. So, if every company you send your script to rejects it, you're not defeated because you're writing a better one and becoming more determined.

> Think – how many obstacles have you placed in front of your protagonist? How did he overcome them? If you can do this for someone who doesn't exist, surely you can do the same for yourself?

LEARN TO PITCH

A pitch is an exciting, concise summary of your story. It is a vitally important selling tool, so below are some pointers to make sure that your pitch packs a punch.

> Remember: you've already written part of your pitch in your logline. You just need to give your 'audience' more tantalizing detail.

1. Always start your pitch with your genre.

2. Give a short, interesting synopsis of your script, highlighting who is the main character, what his/her problem is and how s/he overcomes it.

3. Tantalize your 'audience' by giving them just enough detail to hook them so that they want more information.

4. Try to make the pitch reflect the mood of the film. For example, if your script is a dark comedy, give the audience a darkly comic overview.

5. By the end of the pitch you should have the 'audience' eager to know more.

Example of a pitch

'BLUE NOTES, a contemporary psychological thriller,

explores how a Maltese jazz singer living in London, learns to overcome her traumatic Catholic past, gets rid of a destructive boyfriend through unusual methods, and buys her first successful jazz club in Soho.

In the above pitch, I would want to know what happened to the jazz singer that was traumatic. How did she overcome the trauma? What unusual methods did she use to get rid of the boyfriend? How did she get the money to buy a jazz club? The words 'first' jazz club implies she bought more. (Of course, you must have some interesting, credible answers to such questions.)

Attending pitching sessions

The Raindance Organization runs regular pitching sessions throughout the year. However, they are not for the faint-hearted as they are conducted before an audience of up to 100 people and a panel of well-established producers.

After the pitches, the panel confers and selects the best pitch of the night. The winner takes all the cash and one or two producers will ask to read the script. Here is what Raindance say about their pitching sessions:

> You will pitch to a panel of top British film executives. These are the people who matter. They are the people who buy scripts – they are the people who decide what will be made and what won't. To pitch, just drop £5 in the hat, and the floor is yours. You have two minutes to convince them to read your script or make your film. They can and will gong you off if you are boring – but they must give you two good reasons why.

Tips for attending Raindance

◆ Learn a two-minute/one-minute and ½-minute pitch. This is an incredibly useful exercise as it not only improves your writing skills, but prepares you if Raindance change the length of time you have to pitch at the last moment. (They do this if there are too many 'pitchers'. This always throws the unprepared.)

◆ Make eye contact with the producers and the audience.

◆ Convey your passion about your project. (If you're not passionate about it, why should they be?)

◆ Make your project sound exciting.

◆ Speak clearly.

If you follow these points, you could get your script read by an established producer with powerful industry contacts. The last point 'speak clearly' is very important. I've been to a number of these pitching sessions and some 'pitchers' raced through their pitch so no one could follow their story and others made inaudible pitches, even with a microphone. The way to avoid both of these problems is to practise: practise your pitch on family/friends/ strangers. Look at their eyes and body language. They will tell you more than their lips. Are they hooked? Do they want more of the story? If neither, you need to rewrite your pitch.

Pitching one-to-one

Of course, you could have a one-to-one pitching session with a producer. Here are some tips to prepare you.

◆ Find out as much as you can about the person you're meeting – it's always useful to know who you're dealing with. Have they produced any films you liked in the past? If so then mention them.

- Ask him or her about the project they're working on at the moment, i.e. do some more research and find out what it is.

- Prepare a longer pitch for one-to-one meetings – around ten minutes – and be prepared for questions.

- Look at Elliot Grove's comments on pitching at www.raindance.co.uk.

However, if the thought of pitching in public or private fills you with horror, there are other methods you can use.

RESEARCH

Once your script is polished enough to be sent out, you need to research production companies who are likely to be interested in it.

When researching and selecting your submission list, make sure you target specific producers who are looking for your type of project or have done similar projects in the past. Don't send information about all your projects unless they ask for a CV.

Most film companies say they won't accept non-solicited scripts, so how can you make them solicited? Contact a company via e-mail or letter and include a great pitch to hook them, using a written pitch rather than a verbal one. Once they are interested, they will ask to see your script. It then becomes a solicited script! Great, isn't it?

Using the Internet

A website which is an invaluable tool in finding production companies who produce films similar to yours is www.britfilms.com. You will discover an immensely valuable database with a wealth of information such as:

◆ the British Films Catalogue, which will give you information about British film companies, i.e. their addresses, telephone numbers, e-mail addresses and even synopses of produced films! (Compare them to yours.);

◆ an alphabetical list of directors;

◆ information about the British Council;

◆ a guide to getting development money;

◆ details about co-production agreements;

◆ box office statistics;

◆ book publications which include 'how to get your film funded';

◆ scriptwriting and development agencies;

◆ a guide to the Cannes Film Festival (an interesting way to make industry contacts);

◆ funding information on public funding bodies that could help you depending on where you live, e.g. Screen East, Screen South, North West Vision, etc.

Another database which is invaluable to screenwriters is the International Movie Data Base www.imdb.com. This enormous, valuable database contains information about thousands of films and is free:

♦ genre of films;

♦ production companies;

♦ list of all the cast and crew;

♦ tagline and synopsis of film;

♦ amusing trivia and goofs;

♦ internal and external reviews;

♦ budget and box office figures.

If you subscribe to their full service ($12.95 per month), you can also gain access to contact information for actors, agents, publicists and managers, in-production charts for films and TV shows, a company directory of over 10,000 companies, advanced search options that generate millions of customized reports, entertainment news from the *Hollywood Reporter*, a calendar of theatrical releases, film festivals and events, and message boards for entertainment industry professionals.

Use www.britfilms.com and www.imdb.com regularly – both databases contain valuable information which can help you.

In addition to these resources, use some of the organizations I've listed in Chapter 12 to get to know people in the industry.

APPROACHING DIRECTORS

Why not send your script to a director you admire? Don't know how to contact them? Log onto www.britfilms.co.uk. Click on their database of directors. A long list will appear. Click on a director you like and at the bottom of this page you'll see who his agent is. Send the script to him or her.

APPROACHING ACTORS

Why not send your script to an actor you admire? Don't know who their agent is? Use www.imdb.com or buy *Contacts*. *Contacts* is the essential handbook for anyone searching for an agent or casting director, a theatre or a rehearsal room, a photographer or a voice coach, wigs or props. The 2008 edition contains revised listings for over 5,000 companies, services and individuals across all branches of the industry. It costs £12. Log onto www.spotlight.com for more information.

JOIN SHOOTING PEOPLE

Already mentioned in Chapter 12, Shooting People has a membership of 36,890 in the US and UK. The organization:

- offers daily bulletins which inform members about the latest film news;

- lists jobs for filmmakers;

- has a pitch bulletin once a week where you can post your logline and synopsis (for the UK and US markets);

- has a Resources section which features a variety of film contracts and release forms;

- hosts a Discussion Forum.

If you are feeling isolated as a writer, this organization will make you feel like part of a supportive community.

SEND QUERY E-MAILS/LETTERS

One way of getting under the radar of an organization is to find out who the producer's assistant is and send her an e-mail or query letter. An agent/producer may get more than 60 query letters/e-mails a week, but how many do you think the assistant will get? Send your pitch to her, asking if she thinks her boss might like your material. Remember, a query e-mail or letter should immediately capture their attention with a succinct, interesting pitch.

> Remember: today's assistants are often tomorrow's Heads of Development!

USE AN EDITORIAL SERVICE

The Writers' Workshop
Website: www.writersworkshop.co.uk

This is a UK editorial agency run by writers for writers. They charge £250 to read a full length screenplay. This includes (a) a full report by a professional script editor; (b) the opportunity to discuss your work with your editor; and (c) help in placing your work with an agent (if appropriate). They have good links with leading London agents, so it's worth checking their website.

Initialize Films
Website: www.initializefilms.co.uk

This organisation offers a range of services for screenwriters, filmmakers and producers and their courses are supported by the UK Film Council, Skillset and BBC Film Network. They also run a series of networking events called 'MeetMarkets' where writers and producers meet. Log on to their website for more information and dates.

EUROSCRIPT

Website: www.euroscript.co.uk.

Another UK organization that offers courses on screenwriting, marketing and networking. They also run occasional free networking parties.

FIND A UNIQUE WAY TO HOOK THEM

Think of something unique/unusual to write in your e-mail/letter to increase your chances of getting your script requested, e.g. your target audience, linking your script to successful films.

LEARN PATIENCE

If a producer asks to read your script, be patient after you've submitted it. The producer will usually give it to a script reader who will have an immense amount to read. Wait about six weeks before you call or e-mail the company to ask if they've had time to read the script. If they haven't, a polite reminder could give them the gentle nudge they need to remember to read your script next.

SHOW APPRECIATION

As I mentioned when pitching, find out about a producer's past films. Find at least one you like and mention a small detail from the film which shows you have specifically targeted this producer. Everyone likes to know that their work is appreciated, so tell them.

CULTIVATE CONTACTS

Go to all the networking industry events you can – there are a great many in Europe and the States. They are a great way to make contacts in the industry and to find out who is looking for what.

Here are some networking tips.

1. Print some professional looking business cards to give to people. (And ask for theirs.)

2. Make notes about anything important after the event. (You will forget details a couple of weeks later.)

3. Don't wait for people to speak to you. I know this is difficult if you're shy, but remember – people like talking about themselves. Ask them about their job, their films, their lives. (What producer isn't interested in his films or his life?)

4. Make eye contact. People feel great if you look (and are!) interested in what they have to say. We all know the awful feeling of speaking to a person who's looking at someone he obviously wants to speak with more than you.

5. Be articulate. You're a writer – use effective language.

6. Too often writers moan about agents and producers at networking events. Don't – you'll come across as a whining defeatist. The film world is a small one. People will remember your negativity, not your writing.

7. Don't ignore people in your rush to reach the professionals. You never know who might be standing beside you at the bar.

(One writer I met was standing beside Steven Spielberg at an American Festival!)

8. Do your research about any professionals coming to the event so that when you speak with them you sound like a knowledgeable professional yourself.

9. Go to film screenings – they offer plenty of chances to network.

USE ONLINE SCRIPT SERVICES

In addition to posting your synopsis and logline on Shooting People (for the UK and US markets) you could use online script services such as the following.

Writer's Copyright Association
Website: www.wcauk.com

This UK organization will not only copyright your script, but allow you to post a pitch on its site for NOTHING! You must register with them first, then post your free pitch. It also has a directory of agents.

Litopia Writer's Colony
Website: www.litopia.com

This site was created five years ago by writers. Here's their pitch:

> One of the most useful areas in the Colony is The Pitch Room – a place where members' works-in-progress receive careful analysis and assessment from other members. This is the kind of practical feedback that all writers need, but few ever receive. The quality of criticism here is uniformly high,

and in addition, members find that giving a thoughtful critique of another's work yields tangible benefits to their own writing. Uniquely, members can pitch here directly to leading literary agent Peter Cox. Peter is also freely available in another area of the Colony called Ask the Agent.

Check out the site and see if it interests you.

The Spec Script Library
Website: www.thesource.com/au/scripts

An Australian website with a large database of spec scripts. The Spec Script Library was established in 1997 to connect those who write scripts with those who source scripts. They state that this 'library' is the largest resource of its type in the world.

Project Greenlight
Website: www.projectgreenlight.com

Sponsored by HBO and Miramax, together with series creators Ben Affleck and Matt Damon. Screenwriters compete against thousands of other contestants to be the one screenplay chosen for production by Project Greenlight. The stakes are high, and the screenplay chosen can be the 'make or break' opportunity for the new screenwriter.

USE SCRIPT BROKERAGE COMPANIES
This is how they work: you send them your script plus a fee, they then write a short report called 'coverage' highlighting its marketability (or lack of it) and, depending on what level of service you've paid for, will give you feedback on how to improve it. If the company 'recommends' your script, you will be given a

referral to an agent or producer. However, some not only charge a fee for analysing the script, but also a percentage if your script is sold.

ScriptShark Spec Market
Website: www.scriptshark.com

An American site, ScriptShark believes that the current script submission system is inefficient so they created this service to find new talent outside the usual submission pipeline. ScriptShark is not a literary agency – they don't negotiate sales or options, but they will introduce you to an agent or producer if they recommend your script. However, you will discover that this is not a cheap service. A Coverage Report costs $155. Check out their website to see if it's worth spending this amount of money in the hope of getting your script into the hands of influential producers.

The Pipeline into Motion Pictures
Website: www.scriptpimp.com

An American site. If your script receives a 'Consider' or 'Recommend' in the coverage from Pipeline, their staff will help you polish your script and circulate it to their industry contacts. They currently have over 300 producers who provide them with details of their production agenda. This insider information enables Pipeline to send these producers exactly the type of script they are looking for. They are already working with a dozen new writers in the development of their movie scripts. They also have a database of 1,150 listings of managers, agencies, producers and production companies. You pay $99.95 for a year's membership of this database.

The Writers Agency
Website: www.thescriptagency.com

This is the online version of the Writers Agency in Quebec. They charge 5% if they sell or option your script. There are no fees for writers to post their material in their database, but they don't post every script submitted – they filter the projects for quality.

Script Blaster
Website: www.scriptblaster.com

An American site which states it will e-mail your query letter to 900 producers, managers and agents for $89. Here's what they say:

> We recommend that your query letter be short and to the point, which generally means no longer than a page.
>
> A catchy logline is the key to a query letter's overall effectiveness and should be approximately 25–40 words in length.
>
> A brief synopsis can be included (preferably 2–3 paragraphs), revealing more about the plot, characters and genre. The goal is to create a compelling reason why this story needs to be told! Try to avoid writing overly long paragraphs. It is important to present your query letter in a format that is clear and easy to read.
>
> When disclosing background information about yourself, only put in what's relevant. An award, education, option agreement and produced works can be mentioned, everything else, leave out.

Try to be original, remember your query letter is the first contact a writer makes with the industry and an engaging, well written query can take you far!

Words of caution

One or two of these services might fast-forward your career as a screenwriter, but before your sign up for anything:

1. Make sure that your script is ready for the marketplace.

2. Read the small print on the sites carefully.

Most services offer reduced fees for scripts that you resubmit after polishing them. This can be worthwhile, but be sure your draft is significantly improved before sending it back to them.

ENTERING SCREENWRITING COMPETITIONS

UK Competitions

The British Short Screenplay Competition (BSSC)
Website: www.kaosfilms.co.uk

Kaos Films state that they run the only international short screenplay competition that undertakes to produce the winning screenplays. Three winning screenwriters of BSSC will have their screenplays produced by Kaos Films and each will be premiered at BAFTA (subject to BAFTA availability) and entered into film festivals around the world before being screened in selected cinemas in the UK.

Red Planet Competition
Website: www.redplanetpictures.com

Red Planet Pictures is the production company of writer Tony Jordon. His first competition ran in 2007. Red Planet is committed to discovering new writing talent each year through an annual competition. E-mail the team on redplanetprize@ redplanetpictures.co.uk for details of their next competition.

Euroscript Screen Competition
Website: www.euroscript.co.uk

Euroscript are looking for writers with powerful story ideas and original voices. The writer doesn't have to write a script, only a two-page outline of the story, plus a 10-page writing sample from any script you've written. Entry fee is £35.

> Winners of the Euroscript Screen Story Competition write three drafts of their script within a specified time period. Working one-to-one with a script consultant they receive as much face-to-face and written feedback as is required to complete each of the three drafts. Once each draft is complete, they receive a full script report, usually running to five or six pages, together with an annotated script. At the end of the process they are offered marketing advice.

Previous entrants have come from countries as diverse as Bulgaria, France, New Zealand, Israel, Denmark, Belgium, Ireland, Spain and Hungry. The winning treatment in 2007, *The Lost and Found* by Alexis Roberts, came from South Africa. In 2008, Jessica Davidson's treatment called *This Other Eden* won the competition.

American Competitions
Final Draft Big Break Contest
Website: www.bigbreakcontest.com

An annual competition with $30,000 in cash and prizes. Here are the log lines of three winners of the 2007 competition.

1st Place Winner: Robert Frisbee, CA for *Cityfall*

In a bleak and distant feudal future, the world's last city is dying, choked off within a mysterious energy barrier that cuts it off from the outside world. Humanity's only hope to regain what lies 'beyond the breach' is carried in the heart of a rebellion rising up against the fist and steel of a brutal ruler.

2nd Place Winner: Geraint Horwood, Buckinghamshire, UK for *Knight Knight*

Two saddle-sore knights go on a quest for love, adventure and comfortable underwear. Their quest to save a damsel in distress finds them working for the very King who kidnapped her. The damsel bullies them into rescuing her and soon it is they who are in distress.

3rd Place Winner: Tony Urgo, CA for *The Wizard Joe*

King of a resplendent fairytale country, Leonard Ludwig wakes up to discover he's been in a coma. All his life, he remembers the results of an experimental therapy that kept his mind alive while his body healed. As rival factions threaten to take control of his beloved world, Leonard fights to save the only reality he now knows.

Nicholl Fellowship
Website: www.oscars.org/nicholl

The Nicholl Fellowships in Screenwriting programme is an international competition open to screenwriters who have not earned more than $5,000 writing for film or television. Entry scripts must be the original work of a sole author or of two collaborative authors. Entries must have been written originally in English. Adaptations and translated scripts are not eligible. Up to five $30,000 fellowships are awarded each year. This is what they say about scripts:

> The writer, especially the beginner, needs to love her story, to know it inside and out, and to be passionate about her characters and their problems. When the writer is connected to material in this way, the energy and emotion will more often come through to the reader. And that's the person you have to grab – whether at a contest or in a producer's or an agent's office. If you really care about your story, maybe a reader will too.

Log on to the website for more details.

Scriptapalooza Screenwriting Competition
Website: www.scriptapalooza.com

The Writers' Guild of America (West) and Writers' Guild of Canada endorse this competition which has been running for ten years. Scriptapalooza supports 13 of the top winning writers months after the competition is over. This is what WGC says:

> story-tellers come from all over the world and from all walks of life. Along with offering $10,000 prize money, Scriptapalooza takes the writers to the next level, to provide access to the studios, producers and agencies.

You can enter this American competition online for $40.

American Scriptwriting Competition
Website: www.flatshoe.com

Flatshoe Entertainment state that they want to find the most talented writers from around the world and work with them, offering $12,000 to the winner.

Script Pimp Competition
Website: www.scriptpimp.com

The 2008 Script Pimp Competition is searching for 20 great scripts. They state on their site:

> Each screenplay entered is guaranteed two reads from the Script Pimp panel of judges which is composed of working literary agents, literary managers and development directors from the film industry.

This is an annual screenwriting competition, so if you miss one deadline, start writing for their next one.

Other competitions
You will find many more screenwriting competitions on this site:

www.google.com/Top/Arts/Writers_Resources/Contests/
Screenwriting

ATTEND FILM FESTIVALS
Go to as many film festivals as you can afford and make contacts.

The Cheltenham Film Festival
Website: www.screenwritersfestival.com

This festival is the brainchild of producer David Pearson. The first festival was held in 2006 and has now become an annual event. The festival usually takes place between June and July. Here are some reasons to attend:

- to find out what kind of stories filmmakers are looking for now;

- to meet established filmmakers, writers, agents and managers;

- to improve your writing through workshops;

- to network with peers.

For further information, log onto the website.

The Times BFI Film Festival
Website: www.bfi.org.uk

Held annually: interviews with directors and actors, lively debates and film screenings.

The Edinburgh Film Festival
Website: www.edfilmfest.org.uk

Held in June. Lively. Like the BFI Festival, full of interviews, debates and film screenings.

The Berlin International Film Festival
Website: www.berlinale.de

Held in February. Lively. Eventful. Cold. Take thermal underwear!

The Festival, also known as the Berlinale, has grown to become Berlin's largest cultural event, bringing an unparalleled buzz to town for two weeks in February. More than 19,000 film professionals from 120 countries are accredited for the Berlinale every year. The festival has also become one of the most significant forums and discussion boards for the industry, ranking alongside Cannes and Venice in terms of prestige. Although the Berlinale is best known for its promotion of world cinema and fresh talent, a number of Hollywood classics and big-name directors have won over the juries and claimed the coveted 'Golden Bear' award. (N.B. The bear is the symbol of Berlin.)

The Cannes Film Festival
Held in May. Boisterous. Busy. Blistering. Take some cool clothes and plasters for skinned feet. There's a lot of walking up and down the Croissette. (I got through three boxes of plasters when I went!)

If you can afford it, this is a great way to meet many interesting people and find fantastic parties.

The Venice Film Festival
Held every year in late August or early September on the island of the Lido, Venice. This festival started in 1932 and is the oldest in the world. Here is your chance to see films from well-known directors interspersed with the up-and-coming. The director Ang Lee won the coveted Golden Lion award in 2007 for his film *Caution, Lust*.

Go there if you want to meet interesting people in a seductive setting.

Log on to the www.britfilms.com and www.writersguild.org.uk websites for a guide to going there and how to get accreditation (free if you're a full member of Writers' Guild of Great Britain).

Other Film Festivals

There are many more film festivals around the world. To discover invaluable information about them, log onto the wonderful www.britfilms.com site and discover the large Directory of International Film & Video Festivals. Also try www.indiefilms.com/bag/filmfest.htm for American film festivals.

GETTING AN AGENT

It's incredibly difficult to get an agent interested in your screenwriting if you haven't been produced. However, if you've written a good screenplay and are prepared to market it thoroughly, you will find an interested production company. Use the marketing tools I've shown you in this book, then sign up with the International Movie Data Base for access to the addresses of thousands of production companies.

If you have enough money and you're determined to break into the American market, you could also buy the *Hollywood Creative Directory* to gain more access to companies that would best suit your script. For the American market, you must be prepared to sign a release form. They won't be interested in your script without it. (Log onto www.sonnyboo.com and you will discover a sample release form, along with many other film contracts.)

> **N.B.** *The seven American major studios – Fox, Paramount, Disney, MGM/UA, Universal, Warner Bros, Sony Columbia – won't look at an unrepresented writer without a producer or director attached, so don't waste money sending it to them without any one attached.*

Marketing your work

Even if you do get an agent, you should still market your work. This is a difficult thing for writers to accept. I've heard many writers with agents moan that it's not their job to market their work. Let me tell you why it's important for you to keep marketing. You might be one of fifty clients that the agent or manager already has. He or she won't have as much time as you have to promote your work. Don't complain about this fact – work harder to even the odds in your favour.

Successful screenwriters constantly meet people and make industry contacts. Once you get the interest of one of these contacts, you can then pass them onto your agent who'll negotiate better terms than you can. Can you imagine how great your relationship with your agent will be if you are prepared to market at least some of your work? Think of the knock-on effect. Who is the agent going to ring when a producer contacts them because he wants a good writer? The whinger who complains how little his agent does for him? Or you, the positive professional who is prepared to work hard to achieve success?

Postscript
20 important things to check
before you send out your script

1. Have you presented your story in an original way?

2. Is there foreshadowing of conflict?

3. Do you have a clearly defined protagonist?

4. Does the protagonist have a clear goal or problem?

5. Is the antagonist introduced early and is he/she/it a worthy adversary?

6. Are the characters three-dimensional?

7. Do you need every character you've written? Think why each character is there.

8. Is the dialogue individual to each character?

9. Is the narrative (action) concise, descriptive and visual enough to tell the story?

10. Are the scene transitions smooth?

11. Are the speeches short? (No talking heads or numerous phone calls.)

12. Have you got enough twists and turns to keep the script-reader interested?

13. Has this script been checked for typing mistakes, homophone confusion and spelling errors?

14. Have you erased as many camera directions as you can?

15. Have you written only what can be seen or heard?

16. Have you used the correct script formatting?

17. Does your script evoke an emotional response in the reader?

18. Have you cut out extraneous adverbs and such words as 'while', 'about', 'a little', 'there might be', etc.?

19. Is your story focused, clear-cut and logical?

20. Have you researched the companies you're going to send it to?

Appendix 1
Script Websites

Reading scripts is a vital part of learning to become a great screenwriter. Read as many scripts as you can. You will learn far more from them than from listening to lecturers talk about intellectual theories related to screenwriting.

Below is a large selection of websites to help you.

- www.scriptcrawler.net
  The largest online database of scripts from produced movies. Many have several versions of the script.

- www.simplyscript.com
  Download scripts and adverts about scriptwriting programmes.

- www.awesomemoviescripts.cjb.net
  Large range of online scripts both ancient and modern – from *Gone With the Wind* to *10 Things I Hate About You*.

- http://www.aellea.com
  Range of pre-1970 scripts and film transcripts.

- www.iscriptdb.com
  Large film script database. The site also contains a database of screenwriters and interviews with screenwriters.

- www.script-o-rama.com
  One of the oldest sites for downloading film screenplays.

◆ www.screentalk.org/ezine
  More screenplays to download.

> **N.B.** *Some shooting scripts are production drafts and will have scene numbers. DO NOT number your scenes – leave that job to the production manager.*

Here are more general screenwriting sites that will help you.

◆ www.writing.org.uk
  Robin Kelly's website gives useful information on film, television and radio writing, and also has useful links.

◆ www.wordplay.com
  An interesting site that includes the 'columns' – useful information and advice on aspects of screenwriting (for Hollywood), as well as 'letters' – which add more specific advice. Also includes features written by professional screenwriters, and film and writing forums with a searchable archive.

◆ http://hollywood.com
  News about Hollywood films, fan sites, DVDs, a Weekly Box Office Top Five.

◆ www.sfu.ca/praxis/
  Canadian screenwriting site.

◆ http://screenwriter.com/inside/main
  American screenwriting articles, screenwriting interviews and links.

- www.oscars.org
  Information about the Motion Picture Arts and Sciences.

- http://netspace.net.au/~haze/screen
  Many screenwriting links.

- www.screenwritersutopia.com
  Includes information on forums, interviews, screenwriting contests and articles.

- www.scriptsales.com.
  This site called, Done Deal, informs you about script sales in Hollywood, has interviews, gives advice and provides contact information for agencies and companies.

> **N.B**. *Most of these sites interconnect to other databases to increase their inventory.*

Appendix 2
Screenwriting Software

PC
Celtx
Website: www.celtx.com
Free, open source scriptwriting software. Linux version available.
www.celtx.com

Cinergy Script Editor
Website: www.mindstarprods.com/cinergy/ScriptEditor.html
Free Windows-based script editor program offered in conjunction
with a full suite of non-free production management tools under
the name Cinergy Motion Picture Production System.

DreamaScript
Website: www.dreamascript.com
All-in-one screenwriting software.

Final Draft v. 7
Website: www.finaldraft.com
Allows you to build your story on index cards and then see your
outline as you write your screen-play. But even more amazing
is the fact that you can cut and paste a script into Final Draft
(that hasn't been formatted correctly) and it will reformat it for
you! It will do this whether you are writing a screen-play for film
or TV, TV sitcoms or stage plays. Well worth the money if you
can afford it.

Movie Magic Screenwriter
Website: www.scriptplay.com
Integrated professional screenwriting software.

Practical Scriptwriter
Website: www.practicalscriptwriter.co.uk
Requires no knowledge of script formats.

Scriptbuddy
www.scriptbuddy.com
Web-based screenwriting software.

ScriptRight Mobile Edition
Website: www.scriptright.com
Screenwriting software for Pocket PC and Palm OS.

Sophocles
Website: www.sophocles.net
Windows-based software for feature film and TV screenwriting.
The 2008 version also provides an interface for developing and
maintaining a step outline in conjunction with your screenplay.

Script Smart
Microsoft Word templates. Free! Log onto the BBC's very useful
site called www.bbcwritersroom.co.uk You will see a number of
options in the left-hand column. Click on Script Smart. A window
will open with a new column on the right hand side. Click on
Downloads. Another window will open and you will see a number
of versions of Script Smart. The latest version for Windows is
Script Smart Gold, Version 2. If your computer is up-to-date this
is the version for you. If it's not, down-load Version 1. There are

also versions for Macintosh computers.

> **N.B**. *Matthew Carliss, the creator, has provided an invaluable tool for writers and should be congratulated.*

IBM

Magic Ant Productions specializes in applications for MS Word, including its MagicScript screenplay template, which supports both Word 97 and Word 2000.

Falstaff Productions offers Falstaff.dot for MS Word versions 95 and higher. Programmed in Visual Basic and claiming a variety of impressive abilities, this free screenplay template comes without technical support, although it is updated from time to time to fix bugs or tweak existing features.

MAC

Jeff Young offers two templates for Macintosh Wordperfect 2.1 through 3.5. One is for conventional screenplays based on the Cole and Haag guidelines; the other is for two-column video (A/V) scripts. The templates are stored in Stuffit archives, and free for the price of a download.

Montage Screenwriting Software for Mac OS X
Website: www.marinersoftware.com

Chris Adamson's Screenplay Stylesheet Package for Macintosh, for MS Word 5.0 or greater, Nisus 3.0 or greater, and WriteNow 4.0. As Chris puts it, these are 'Freeware (but not "public domain")'.

If you are strapped for cash, go for Matthew Carliss' free Script Smart at the BBC Writer's Room. If you've come into some money, I'd recommend Final Draft.

Appendix 3
Options and Assignments

BASIC STRUCTURE

Option

A producer will normally enter into an option agreement with the owner of the copyright in a novel or a screenplay. The producer has a period of time – the option period – in which to develop the work and arrange for a script (or even just further drafts, synopses, treatments, etc.) to be written. The producer has until the end of the option period to decide whether they want to buy the rights in the work for the purposes of making their film. If so, the producer and the copyright owner enter into another agreement – the assignment.

Assignment

The terms of the assignment are negotiated at the same time as the terms of the option in order to avoid any dispute as to what exactly it is that the producer receives upon assignment. Under the assignment, the copyright owner assigns to the producer the copyright and other rights necessary for the producer to make a film. The producer may well want to do more than this, for example by exploiting ancillary rights, and will have to negotiate these extra rights.

In return, the copyright owner can expect to receive a fee for the option period and then a further fee upon assigning the rights to the producer.

OPTION PERIOD

The length of the option period varies and will depend on what the producer and the copyright owner agree. It is common for option periods to be between six months and two years long. The producer may also negotiate to have an extension period giving them more flexibility if their plans are behind schedule or they simply want more time. Again, the length is for the parties to agree and it is common for the producer to have to pay a further fee for the extension.

WHAT CAN A PRODUCER DO DURING THE OPTION PERIOD?

A producer will need consent to develop the work and any rights in the work during the option period. Development usually means commissioning or writing treatments, scripts, plots, character summaries, creating new stories and plots, giving copies of the development materials to third parties such as potential financiers, actors, directors, etc. as well as anything else the producer thinks might be required. A producer will want to be able to develop the work in order to make a film without having to go back to the copyright owner for permission to do a particular activity.

The producer will also want to know that the copyright owner is not going to let anybody else use the work for the same purposes. The point about having an option is that it should be exclusive throughout the option period and that the copyright owner will not do anything to the work which would prevent the producer from exercising the option if he wants to. The copyright owner should also warrant that he has the right to enter into the option and the assignment. If you think that the copyright owner might not have the rights you need or if you think that you might need the permission of anyone else then you must try and find out. If in doubt then seek independent legal advice. If there are problems at a later date then it will be more difficult to raise independent finance and find a distributor for your film.

PAYMENT STRUCTURE

The payment structure (or whether there should be any payment at all) and the amounts are both very much open to negotiation between the parties. Although there is a payment structure used by many producers it is by no means set in stone. The following is only a guideline.

The copyright owner can expect a fee for granting an option period, particularly if the option is exclusive – the option fee. If the producer wants to extend the option period then the copyright owner may expect a further fee. The producer will normally have to pay a further fee on the completion of the assignment – the exercise fee. The option fee is often paid 'on account of' the exercise fee which means that the amount of the option fee is taken off the amount of the exercise fee to be paid. (This may not be the case with the option extension fee.)

The exercise fee itself can sometimes be on account of a percentage of the final budget of the film – the principal photography fee.

The definition of final budget will have to be agreed at the outset. The producer should also consider setting a cap on the principal photography fee but should expect the copyright owner to negotiate a minimum. The final budget may be much larger than anticipated and therefore the producer could end up paying the copyright owner much more. This fee is usually paid on the first day of principal photography of the film. If both parties think that the film is likely to be made and that it will be a commercial success and the copyright owner is able to negotiate such a position, the producer may offer the copyright owner a share of any profits from the film. From the producer's perspective, it is important to make it clear what the copyright owner will be entitled to and, just as importantly, when they will receive it. Should the share be in gross profits or net profits? Should the share be in all of the net profits of the film or just the producer's share of such net profits? What expenses will be taken off before what is left can be called 'profit'? Quite often, both parties agree that whatever term they use shall be defined in accordance with the principal financing and distribution documents for the sake of consistency and to avoid protracted negotiations at such an early stage in the life of the film.

HOW DO I EXERCISE AN OPTION?

The terms of the option should set this out but the most common method is that the producer gives written notice to the copyright owner. Both parties should then sign the assignment and any payments that might have to be made on exercise of the option are made at this point.

WHAT IS A TURNAROUND PROVISION?

Turnaround provisions are normally found in assignments of rights of underlying works. If the producer has exercised the option but has not started making a film within a specified period of time, then the copyright owner might want to have the rights to make the film back, so that they can allow someone else to try. From a producer's perspective, it is common to negotiate a provision that if the copyright owner wants the rights back then they will have to pay for them. The amount is certainly negotiable and many producers expect to be reimbursed for all of the money they paid in order to buy the rights (excluding the initial option fees), as well as the cost of developing them.

Reed Smith Richards Butler LLP is a limited liability partnership registered in England (registered no. OC303620) with its registered office at Beaufort House, Tenth Floor, 15 St Botolph Street, London EC3A 7EE, England. Reed Smith Richards Butler LLP is regulated by the Solicitors Regulation Authority.

Appendix 4
A Sample Option Agreement (UK)

Writer's Agreement

Dated: [   ]

Producer: [   ] ('**the Producer**')

Address: [   ]

Writer: [   ] ('**the Writer**')

Address: [   ]

Script Title: [   ] ('**the Work**')

1. **Subject of the Agreement**
   1.1 Subject to the terms of this Agreement the Writer
   undertakes to grant to the Producer the right to use the
   Work for the creation of a film
   1.2 In consideration thereof the Producer undertakes to pay
   the writer the remuneration agreed herein

2. **Revision**
   2.1 The parties agree on a revision of the Work as follows:
   2.1.1 [Version 1: the Writer will undertake the

amendments himself and will deliver the revised
work by (date)]

2.1.2 [Version 2: the Producer is entitled to entrust the
revision to a co-writer. The revised work must be
submitted to the original writer who alone can
decide if his name can continue to be used]

2.2 If the producer relinquishes in writing the right to use the
Work, the Writer is entitled to use it for other purposes
even before expiry of the deadline laid down in Article
3.6. In this case the Producer is entitled to reimbursement
of half the remuneration agreed in Article 4.1

3. Rights in the Work

3.1 The Writer guarantees to the Producer that he has all the
rights in the work mentioned and releases the Producer
from any claim from third parties on the rights to the
script

3.2 For a period of fifteen years from the contract date the
Writer exclusively assigns to the Producer the right to
publish the Work to use it to make a film and to translate
it and reproduce it for that purpose. It does not include
the authorisation to create another work of the same kind
after the film has been released (re-make)

3.3 The Producer is entitled to adapt the script to the extent
that the particular conditions of an audio-visual work
require. Any modifications must not be detrimental to the
message and character of the work. The revisions as far
as possible must be carried out in agreement with the
writer. The title to the film does not necessarily have to
correspond to the title of the script

3.4 The parties agree that [the direction of the film will be
entrusted to (name)] or [the Producer is free to choose the

director of the film]

3.5 The Writer exclusively grants to the Producer an unlimited right:

3.5.1 To rework the film (to make different versions);

3.5.2 To translate it from the original version by post-synchronization (dubbing) or sub-titling;

3.5.3 To copy it on video tape or any other data medium;

3.5.4 To make it available to the public, to dispose of it or circulate it in any manner whatsoever;

3.5.5 To present it, project it, or have it seen or heard in any manner whatsoever;

3.5.6 To transmit it on television or similar means, to re-transmit it so as to have the work seen or heard;

3.5.7 To use characters, photos etc, appearing in the film for other commercial purposes (merchandising);

3.5.8 To incorporate the work into a multimedia product and release it;

3.5.9 The Writer retains any other rights in the work.

3.6 The Producer is not obliged to use all the rights granted to him under this Agreement. However, if within [five] years from the date of signing the Agreement, the Producer has not used the Work to create an audio-visual work (film) and shooting has not yet even begun, all the rights granted under this Agreement revert to the Writer without compensation being due from either party.

3.6.1 The Producer is authorised to extend this period to a maximum of [eight] years. He must give notice in writing of this to the Writer before the expiry of the [five-year] period. In this case he must grant the Writer additional remuneration amounting to [ ]% of the basic remuneration specified in Article 4.1, per year extended.

3.7 The Writer is entitled to be named in the usual form and order in the credits at the beginning and/or end of the film as well as in any advertising for the film

4. **Remuneration**

4.1 The Producer undertakes to pay the Writer £[ ], to be paid as follows:

4.2 £[ ] at the conclusion of the contract and £[ ] on acceptance of the revised version;

4.3 In addition the Writer will be reimbursed for the following expenses [list];

4.4 In respect of all other exploitation income the writer is entitled to [ ]% of net receipts to the extent that these exceed the total remainder of the production budget not covered (producer's investment) and the amount representing the production costs in excess of the budget which are payable by the Producer.

4.4.1 The amounts collected by the Producer are considered as net receipts for the purposes of this clause, after deduction of:

4.4.1.1 Any commission from the seller up to a maximum of [25]% paid to an agent or distributor;

4.4.1.2 Declared costs for film print, sub-titling or synchronization;

4.4.1.3 Declared costs for transport, insurance, customs and revenue taxes;

4.4.1.4 Declared costs borne by the Producer for advertising relating to the film's exploitation.

4.5 If the Producer looks after the sale himself he can claim the amount of the seller's commission

4.6 If the Writer publishes a derivative prose work based on the Work created within the terms of the Agreement, the Producer is entitled to [a fifth] of the net profit. Publication of the prose cannot be made until after the film has been released. Article 3.5 is reserved

4.7 Awards and prizes, which are explicitly given to the script, will be given to the Writer

4.8 At the end of each calendar year the Producer will prepare a schedule of expenses and income from the exploitation of the film. He will automatically present this to the Writer and pay the amount due to him no later than the end of the following March. The Producer undertakes to keep proper accounts of the exploitation of the film and allow the Writer or trustee duly appointed by him to have access to accounting records and supporting documents

5. Other Provisions

5.1 The parties mutually undertake to make available the necessary documents for the application of the rights arising from this contract

5.2 Any amendment to this contract must be in writing

5.3 The Artist shall keep as confidential the provisions of and any information which may come to the Artist's attention in connection with this agreement

5.4 This agreement is governed by and construed in accordance with the laws of England and subject to the exclusive jurisdiction of the Courts of England

Signed _____ [Writer]   Dated _____

Signed _____ [Producer] Dated _____

There are many variations on this option agreement. The important point to remember is that all agreements should be checked by a solicitor before you sign.

Appendix 5
Sample Option Agreement (USA)

_____

Title of screenplay

_____

Author

_____

Producer

This letter, when signed and dated by you, _____,
and returned by mail to me, _____, will confirm the
agreement between you and I regarding any and all motion
picture, television, broadcast, home video, remake, sequel, CD-
Rom and all other computer-assisted forms of media,
merchandising, allied, subsidiary and ancillary rights now known
or hereafter invented throughout the universe and in any and all
languages (exclusive of book publishing) to the screenplay written
by you called _____.

OPTION

In return for $_____, development services and other valuable
consideration, receipt of which is hereby acknowledged, you
hereby grant me the exclusive option to purchase the Rights to
the screenplay for an exclusive period of ___ months from the

date of my receipt of this signed contract. It is also agreed that the option may be automatically extended without any additional consideration at the end of ___ months for an additional ___ days by giving notice if there are negotiations with a buyer in order to conclude negotiations. The option may be extended on the same terms for an additional ___ months upon mutual written consent.

If the property is set up with a production company, the option may be automatically extended for a period of ___ months upon notice and payment to you of $_____. Thereafter, the option may be extended for an additional ___ months upon notice and payment to you of $_____.

PURCHASE PRICE

1. Theatrical Motion Picture
If the initial release is a theatrical motion picture, the purchase price is __% of the 'direct approved budget' (i.e. excluding legal, interest, contingency, overhead, and completion guarantees) with a floor of $_____ and a ceiling of $_____.

2. Television Movie
Network: If the initial release is a television movie for a network, the purchase price is $_____.

Cable: If the initial release is a television movie for a cable or non-network broadcast, the purchase price is $_____.

3. Sequels, Prequels, Spinoffs
50% of original.

4. Remakes
$33^{1}/_{3}$% of original

5. Television series

For a broadcast network, prime time series, payments will be $_____ per produced episode of up to 30 minutes; $_____ per produced episode up to 60 minutes; $_____ over 60 minutes.

For a series on any other broadcast or cable entity, payments will be $_____ up to 30 minutes; $_____ up to 60 minutes; $_____ over 60 minutes.

WRITING SERVICES

Any additional writing services shall be paid according to appropriate trade/guild minimums.

PROFIT PARTICIPATION

___% of 100% of net profits from all sources to _____(Production Company).

You warrant that you, _____, have (a) exclusive 100% ownership of the Rights free and clear of any claim, right, adverse interest or encumbrance and (b) the authority and unencumbered right to enter into this Agreement and grant the Rights to me.

Until such time as we execute a more detailed document incorporating these and other provisions standard for such agreements in the entertainment industry, this will constitute an agreement binding on _____ and _____ and their respective successors, assigns, heirs, and legal representatives.
_____ (Producer) shall consult with you or your representative regarding the assignment of the Agreement but shall have at her sole discretion the right to assign this Agreement or any of her rights hereunder, but no such assignment shall

relieve her of her obligations hereunder unless the assignee assumes all such obligations in writing.

This Agreement constitutes the entire understanding between us with respect to the subject matter hereof and no modification of this Agreement shall be effective unless it is in writing executed by us both. Nothing contained herein shall be deemed to create or constitute a partnership between or joint venture by us. This Agreement shall be construed in accordance with the laws of the State of _____ applicable to contracts negotiated, executed, and to be wholly performed within said state. Reference to _____ (producer) shall include _____(production company) and conversely.

ACCEPTED AND AGREED:

_____
Name

_____
Date

_____
Name

_____
Date

There are many variations on this option agreement. The important point to remember is that all agreements should be checked by a solicitor before you sign.

A Glossary of Common Screen Terms

The most useful terms you are likely to encounter are given below. There are more!

Action – The moving pictures we see on screen. Also, the direction given by a director indicating that filming begins.

Above-the-line – The costs that occur before filming; this includes salaries of the talent and creative team (director, producer, screenwriter), plus any rights required for adapted scripts.

Against – A term describing the ultimate potential pay for a writer in a film deal. $50,000 against $200,000 means that the writer is paid $50,000 when the script is finished (through rewrite and polish); when and if the movie goes into production, the writer gets an additional $200,000.

Alan Smithee – A fictional name taken by a writer or director who doesn't want their real name credited on a film.

Angle – A particular camera position.

Attached – Agreement by named actors and/or a director to be a part of the making of a movie.

Audio/visual script – A dual column screenplay with video description on the left and audio and dialogue on the right, used in advertising, corporate videos, documentaries and training films.

B.G. – Abbreviation for 'background' (i.e. 'In the B.G., kids are fighting').

Back end – Payment on a movie project when profits are realized.

Back story – Experiences of a main character taking place prior to the main action, which contribute to character motivations and reactions.

Beat – Used to indicate some (beat) hesitation on the part of a character and placed in brackets.

Beat sheet – An abbreviated description of the main events in a screenplay.

Brads – Brass fasteners used to bind a screenplay printed on three-hole paper. Used in America.

Breakdown script – Detailed list of all items, people, props, etc. required for a shoot on a day-by-day basis.

CGI – Computer generated imagery, a term denoting that computers will be used to generate the full imagery.

Character arc – The emotional progress of the characters during the story.

Cheat a script – Fudging the margins and spacing of a screenplay on a page (usually with a software program) in an attempt to fool the reader into thinking the script is shorter than it really is. (Don't do this – they won't be fooled!)

Cinema verité – This literally means: 'cinema truth.' A documentary style in which no directorial control is exerted.

Close up (C.U.) – A very close camera angle on a character or object.

Continuing dialogue – Dialogue spoken by the same character that continues uninterrupted onto the next page, marked with a (cont'd).

Continuous action – Included in the scene heading when moving from one scene to the next, as the action continues.

Copyright – Placing under your Name on the Title Page of a script. (However, you don't need to do this – see Chapter 13).

Development – The process of preparing a script for production.

Director's cut – Cut of a movie without studio interference as the director would like it to be seen. The director's cut of *Blade*

Runner is far more interesting than earlier versions, for example.

Dissolve – Editing technique in which the images of one shot is gradually replaced by the images of another.

Dual dialogue – When two characters speak simultaneously, dialogue is written side by side.

Editing – Reconstructing the sequence of events in a movie.

Editor – Individual who performs editing (in consultation with the director) on a movie.

Establishing shot – A cinematic shot that establishes a certain location or area.

Executive producer – Producer who is not involved in any technical aspects of the filmmaking process, but who is still responsible for the overall production, usually handling business and legal issues.

Exposition – Any information about the characters or plot that the audience needs to understand the story. (Scatter vital pieces of information throughout the script, and don't write long passages on one page.)

Extension – A technical note placed directly to the right of the character name that denotes how the character's voice is heard. For example, O.S. is an extension that means off-screen; V.O. is an extension that means voice over.

F.G. – Abbreviation for 'foreground' (i.e. 'In the F.G., women are talking').

First look deal – An arrangement which allows the studio the first right of refusal on purchasing and or producing a project it is interested in. If the studio passes, the project can then be shown to other interested parties.

Flashback – A scene from the past that interrupts the action to explain motivation or reaction of a character to the immediate scene.

Flashforward – A scene that breaks the chronological continuity of the main narrative by depicting events which happen in the future.

Focus group – A small group of people (members of the public not connected with the film) who attend a preview and then offer feedback to producers before further editing.

Freeze frame – The image on the screen stops, freezes and becomes a still shot.

Green light – When a script gets the final approval to proceed with making the project. This is usually given once a final budget is approved (though sometimes the rewrite of a script might affect this along with a certain actor or actress agreeing to be in the project).

High concept – An idea that is felt to have tremendous public appeal, that is commercially appealing. Usually associated with big blockbuster films but can refer to any idea or script that appears to have great potential.

Hip pocket – A casual relationship with an established agent in lieu of a signed, formal agreement of representation.

Hook – A term borrowed from songwriting that describes that thing that catches the public's attention and keeps them interested in the flow of a story.

Indie – Short for independent. Can refer to a film or production company that works outside of the Hollywood/studio system, i.e. a production company independent of major film studio financing.

Intercut – A script instruction denoting that the action moves back and forth between two or more scenes.

Interrupt – Use a dash – to show that one character is interrupting another.

Locked pages – A term for finalized screenplay pages that are handed out to the department heads and talent in preparation for production.

Logline – A '25 words or less' description of a screenplay.

Master shot – Wide shot that incorporates the entire scene from start to end.

Match cut – A transition from one scene to another matching the same or a similar subject within the frame

Montage – A cinematic device used to show a series of scenes, all related and building to some conclusion.

M.O.S. – This is the abbreviation used if a scene is to be shot mute. (I love the story of how this odd script direction came about. Apparently, in the early days of sound pictures, a German director bellowed through a megaphone: 'Mit Out Sound' and the phrase stuck!)

Multiple casting – When an actor plays more than one character.

Notes – Ideas about a screenplay given to a screenwriter (usually by the producer) which the writer is expected to use to revise the screenplay.

Numbered scenes – Numbers that appear to the right and left of the scene heading to aid the assistant director in breaking down the scenes for scheduling and production.

O.C. – Abbreviation for off camera, denoting that the speaker is in the scene but not seen by the camera.

Opening credits – On-screen text describing the most important people involved in the making of a movie.

Option – The securing of the rights to a screenplay for a given length of time. You should get money for an option.

O.S. – Abbreviation for off screen, denoting that the speaker is not in the scene.

Package – The assembly of the basic elements necessary to secure financing for a film.

PAN – A camera direction indicating a stationary camera that pivots back and forth or up and down.

Pass – A rejection of a script.

Pitch – To verbally 'sell' your script to a potential buyer by making it sound exciting.

Points – Percentage participation in the profits of a film.

Polish – In theory, to rewrite a few scenes in a script to improve them. In practice, a screenwriter is often expected to do a complete rewrite of a script for the price of a polish.

Post-production – Work performed on a movie after the end of principal photography.

POV – Point of view – a camera angle placed so it seems that the camera is the eyes of a character.

Pre-production – Arrangements made before the start of filming: script editing, set construction, location scouting and casting.

Principal photography – The filming of major or significant components of a movie which involve lead actors.

Production bonus – Cash bonus given to the writer of a screenplay who receives shared or sole 'Screenplay by' or 'Written by' credit when the screenplay is turned into a film.

Production manager – Individual responsible for the practical matters such as ordering equipment, getting near-location accommodations for the cast and crew, etc.

Production schedule – Detailed plan of the timing of activities associated with the making of a movie; of particular interest to the production manager.

Production script – A script in which no more major changes or rewrites is anticipated to occur which is used day by day for filming on a movie set.

Public domain – The state in which the creator of a work loses the copyright on it through the passage of the copyright period, failure to renew the work or problems with the original registration of the work with the copyright office.

Property – Any intellectual property in any form (including a play or screenplay) that might form the basis of a movie.

Query – A method of submission in which a writer approaches a production company with a brief, 'hooking' letter, accompanied by a synopsis and sample pages. (If the company accepts e-mails, it's obviously quicker and cheaper to use them.)

Release – A legal document given to unrepresented writers for signing by agents, producers or production companies, absolving said entities of legal liability.

Reversal – A place in the plot where a character achieves the opposite of his aim. This could be bad or good for them, depending on what you are trying to achieve.

Revised pages – Changes are made to the script after the initial circulation of the production script, which are different in colour and incorporated into the script.

Scene heading – Centred, all CAPS heading at the start of an act or scene. Act numbers are written in roman numerals, scene numbers in ordinals.

Shooting schedule – Production schedule for shooting a film with the scenes from a script grouped together and ordered with production considerations in mind.

Shooting script – Script from which a film is made that includes scene numbers, camera angles, inserts and certain input from the director/cinematographer.

Spec script – A script written without being commissioned on the speculative hope that it will be sold.

SPFX – Abbreviation for special effects.

Split screen – A screen with different scenes taking place in two or more sections; the scenes are usually interactive, as in the depiction of two sides of a phone conversation.

Stock shot – A sequence of film previously shot and available for purchase and use from a film library.

Submission – Name for a script once it is submitted to producers or agents.

SUPER – Abbreviation for 'superimpose', meaning the laying of one image on top of another, usually words over a filmed scene (i.e. 'Scotland, 1926').

Synopsis – One- or two-page description of a screenplay.

Tag – A short scene at the end of a movie that usually provides some release of tension from the climax.

Title design – How the title of a movie is displayed on screen.

Transition – For example, DISSOLVE TO: means the action seems to blur and refocus into another scene, and is generally used to denote a passage of time.

Treatment – A scene-by-scene description of a screenplay, minus all or most of the dialogue.

Unsolicited script – A method of script submission in which the writer sends the script, without prior contact, to a production company. (Not advisable.)

V.O. – Abbreviation for voice over, denoting that the speaker is narrating the action onscreen.

WGA signatory – An agent, producer or production company that has signed an agreement to abide by established agreements with the Writers Guild of America.

Writers' Guild of America – Also known as 'WGA'. The main union for screenwriters in the United States, with offices in Los Angeles and New York.

Writers' Guild of Great Britain. Also known as 'WGGB'. The union for writers in Great Britain. Unagented writers can get their contracts vetted by lawyers for nothing if they become members! (Not many people know that.)

Zoom – Shot in which the magnification of the object by the camera's lens is increased (zoom in) or decreased (zoom out/back).

Famous Last Lines

'...and I thought of that old joke, you know, the, this, this guy goes to a psychiatrist and says, "Doc, uh, my brother's crazy, he thinks he's a chicken," and uh, the doctor says, "Well why don't you turn him in?" And the guy says, "I would, but I need the eggs." Well, I guess that's pretty much now how I feel about relationships. You know, they're totally irrational and crazy and absurd and – but uh, I guess we keep going through it...because...most of us need the eggs.' (*Annie Hall*, 1977)

'The greatest trick the Devil ever pulled was convincing the world he didn't exist. And like that, he's gone.' (*The Usual Suspects*, 1995)

'Where you headed, cowboy?
'Nowhere special.'
'Nowhere special. I always wanted to go there.'
'Come on.'   (*Blazing Saddles*, 1974)

'You have no idea what I'm talking about, I'm sure. But don't worry – you will someday.' (*American Beauty*, 1999)

'There are eight million stories in the naked city. This has been one of them.' (*The Naked City*, 1948)

'This is the end! The absolute end!' (*The Lady in the Dark*, 1944)

Index